Britain's finest hour
SPITFIRE

Nigel Cawthorne

Britain's finest hour
SPITFIRE

Nigel Cawthorne

Abbeydale Press

This edition is published by Abbeydale Press,
an imprint of Anness Publishing Ltd,
Blaby Road, Wigston, Leicestershire LE18 4SE
Email: info@anness.com
Web: www.hermeshouse.com; www.annesspublishing.com

Anness Publishing has a new picture agency outlet for images for publishing,
promotions or advertising. Please visit our website www.practicalpictures.com for
more information.

Produced for Anness Publishing Ltd by Editorial Developments, Edgmond, Shropshire
Design: Bacroom Design and Advertising, Birmingham
Index: Marie Lorimer Indexing Services, Harrogate

ETHICAL TRADING POLICY
Because of our ongoing ecological investment programme, you, as our customer, can
have the pleasure and reassurance of knowing that a tree is being cultivated on your
behalf to naturally replace the materials used to make the book you are holding.
For further information about this scheme, go to www.annesspublishing.com/trees

© Anness Publishing Ltd 2011

A CIP catalogue record for this book is available from the British Library.

PUBLISHER'S NOTE
Although the advice and information in this book are believed to be accurate
and true at the time of going to press, neither the authors nor the publisher
can accept any legal responsibility or liability for any errors or omissions
that may have been made.

Contents

Introduction

The Spitfire is an iconic plane. It is a symbol of British – and Allied – resistance to Hitler. It is also a thing of beauty. Designed by Reginald Mitchell, who died of cancer a year before the plane went into service with the RAF, its elliptical wing with a thin cross section gave it a top speed higher than that of the Hawker Hurricane. It became the plane most closely associated with the Battle of Britain, though more Hurricanes fought and bore the brunt of the battle against the Messerschmitt Bf 109.

Mitchell's 1931 design was developed to meet the Air Ministry's specification for a modern fighter capable of 250 miles per hour. The contract was won by the Gloster Gladiator biplane. But Mitchell's design was developed further and the plane first flew in 1934. The name was suggested by the director of Vickers-Armstrong, Sir Robert MacLean, who called his daughter a "little spitfire".

The plane was one of a new generation of all-metal, low-wing fighters. Taking advantage of the techniques of monocoque construction, it was built around 19 frames. The distinctive elliptical wing shape allowed the wings to be very thin, reducing drag. A powerful Rolls-Royce Merlin engine was added along with a closed cockpit, oxygen equipment and four wing-mounted machine guns. A new specification written around the aircraft was formulated in 1935 and the new prototype took to the air on 6 March 1936.

Production facilities were set up across the country, but by May 1940 not a single Spitfire had been completed and the Air Ministry stepped in. In June, the first ten rolled off the production line, just in time for the Battle of Britain which began the following month. The plane continued in service in all theatres throughout the war.

By 1943, tests were being made to see whether the Spitfire could breach the sound barrier. Twenty-four variants were built before the Spitfire was taken out of service in 1957. There are some 44 airworthy Spitfires still flying around the world and a number of prominent memorials.

"The gratitude of every home in our Island, in our Empire, and indeed throughout the world, except in the abodes of the guilty, goes out to the British airmen who, undaunted by odds, unwearied in their constant challenge and mortal danger, are turning the tide of the world war by their prowess and by their devotion. Never in the field of human conflict was so much owed by so many to so few. All hearts go out to the fighter pilots, whose brilliant actions we see with our own eyes day after day."

Winston Churchill – House of Commons, 18 June 1940

Right: German soldiers prepared for Operation Sealion, the amphibious invasion of Britain. But first they needed air supremacy – which the Spitfire would deny them.

Chapter 1

Its Finest Hour

By July 1940, the German armies had taken Norway, the Low Countries and France. The British Army had been rescued from the beaches of Dunkirk. Hitler's forces were now massing on the French coast ready to launch a seaborne invasion of Britain in what he called Operation Sealion. The gold from the Bank of England had already been sent to San Francisco. The Crown Jewels, which cannot legally leave the country, had been buried, because Prime Minister Winston Churchill feared that, if the Germans once set foot on English soil, Britain would be overrun in a matter of weeks.

Right: *Hitler was assured that his air force was invincible. But in the skies above Britain, the Luftwaffe met its match.*

Below: In the late summer of 1940, the head of the Luftwaffe, Reichsmarschall Hermann Göring, visited the beaches of northern France where you can see the coastline of England across the Channel. The Spitfire would prevent him and his Nazi cohorts crossing that narrow body of water.

Above: *Prime Minister Winston Churchill enjoyed watching the air battles. Despite the danger, he would climb to the top of government buildings to see the RAF in action.*

Left: By April 1941, Hitler had realised that the planes of Göring's Luftwaffe were no match for the Spitfire and had shelved the invasion of Britain. With Keitel and Himmler, shown here in the rear, he was planning his disastrous attack on Russia.

But before any invasion could begin, the German Luftwaffe would first have to establish air superiority over the invasion beaches. Its commander Hermann Göring assured Hitler that this would be easy. What he did not know was that the British had finally sorted out their production problems with the Supermarine Spitfire. So, when the Luftwaffe began its attempt to dominate the skies over southern Britain, it found itself up against an enemy with superior equipment.

Below: Spitfire Mark IAs of 610 Squadron based at Biggin Hill, Kent, patrol the skies over England, denying the airspace to the Luftwaffe.

The beginning of the Battle of Britain is generally set at 10 July 1940. On that day nine-tenths of Britain was hidden under heavy cloud and there was driving rain, so most RAF fighter pilots took the opportunity to turn over and have a much needed lie-in. The Germans also made the most of the cloud cover to make photo-reconnaissance flights over possible targets. The Dornier 17 light bombers that made these flights usually suffered heavy losses, but as there were no "scramble" calls that dawn the Luftwaffe enjoyed the freedom of the skies at first light.

Eventually, at 0730 hours (7.30am), 66 Squadron, Spitfires based at Coltishall in Norfolk, got a "scramble" after the radar station at West Beckham had picked up a blip on the radar. One section took off into the driving rain. It was led by Pilot Officer Charles Cook. They climbed through the thick cloud and broke out into brilliant sunshine at around 10,000 feet. Cook was given a bearing to where the enemy aircraft was last spotted. In the early stages of the war Britain's development of radar gave the RAF the upper hand.

Below: *Immediately before World War II, radar had been developed. The RAF used this to identify incoming enemy aircraft and send Spitfires and other fighters to intercept them.*

Right: Once incoming enemy aircraft had been identified, RAF fighter pilots "scrambled". They ran to their planes and took off to take care of the intruders.

Below: Heavy German bombers made easy targets for the agile Spitfires.

At 0815 hours, 66 Squadron finally spotted the enemy, a lone Dornier 17 on a reconnaissance mission. As the Spitfires peeled off one by one, the Dornier started weaving and sliding in an attempt to evade the gunfire from the Spitfires. The gunners in the Dornier fired back, hitting Pilot Officer Cook's windscreen. The hole in the canopy let in cold air. Then one of the Spitfires came up from underneath firing at the Dornier with all eight Brownings blazing. As it closed, the Dornier went into a banking glide. Streaming smoke, it hit the sea between Yarmouth and Harwich. A couple of hours later, the three Spitfire pilots of Pilot Officer Cook, Pilot Officer Studd and Sergeant Robertson landed back at Coltishall to celebrate their success, swap notes and discuss tactics.

Below: *French pilots who had joined the RAF after the fall of France in June 1940 scramble for their Spitfires to continue the fight in the skies above England.*

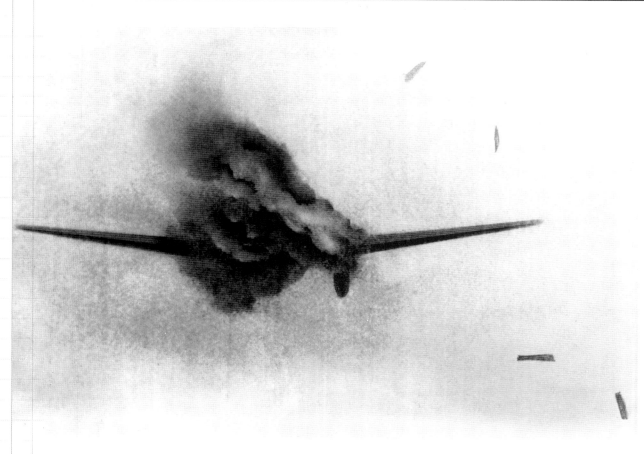

By 1030 hours, 74 Squadron – the Spitfires based at Hornchurch – was scrambled to intercept a Dornier with an escort of over 20 Messerschmitt Bf 109s that were closing in on a convoy coming up the Channel. As they attacked the Dornier, two Spitfires were hit, but not put out of action, by the highly manoeuvrable 109s. The damaged Spitfires continued their attack, hitting the Dornier before they were forced to return to Hornchurch. The remaining four Spitfires continued the fight, hitting a 109, but only inflicting slight damage. As the Spitfires returned to base, 610 Squadron – more Spitfires based at Gravesend – took over, as the enemy was reinforced by another 12 aircraft. The Spitfires scored no more hits. However, they forced the Luftwaffe back to France, while one of the Spitfires from 610 Squadron was damaged and had to make a forced landing at Hawkinge in Kent.

Right: *The Spitfires were not always victorious. This tangled piece of wreckage is the remains of one shot down over the River Medway. Fortunately, the pilot managed to bail out.*

At 1350 hours, British radar picked up a strong signal from a German formation crossing the French coast just west of Calais. This was the largest number of bombers yet seen over the Channel and it was clear that they planned to attack the convoy. The main force was 24 Dornier 17s spread in three groups, with 30 Messerschmitt Bf 110s and more than 20 109s escorting them. Hornchurch scrambled the Spitfires of 74 Squadron, while Hurricanes were sent from Manston, Biggin Hill and Croydon. The base at Kenley in Shropshire sent out six Spitfires of 64 Squadron in the closing stages of the battle.

Above: *Messerschmitt 109s over the English Channel. They would have been spotted by radar and their position and direction would already have been plotted. Within minutes they would be intercepted by Fighter Command.*

In the ensuing dogfight, Flying Officer J. Mungo-Park's Spitfire downed a Dornier. Another Spitfire of 74 Squadron hit one of the 109s, sending it back to France. The Dornier formation broke up. Two Dorniers were shot down along with ten of the escort fighters. Four Spitfires and three Hurricanes were damaged. There was only one British fatality. While downing a Dornier, Flying Officer Tom Higgs of 111 Squadron collided with it, knocking the wing off his Hurricane. He crashed into the sea and was not recovered. However, the convoy continued on its way, having lost only one ship.

Below: *Spitfires also had to protect the Royal Navy, guarding the English Channel and the convoys that passed through it against air attack.*

Above: *Plotters of the Women's Auxiliary Air Force in the operations room of the headquarters of Number 11 Group at Uxbridge in Middlesex, where they plotted the incoming German planes and directed the RAF interceptors.*

Right: *Flight Sergeant G.C. "Grumpy" Unwin of Number 19 Squadron climbing out of his Mark 1 Spitfire at Fowlmere in Cambridgeshire after a sortie. Between May and September 1940, he shot down over 14 enemy planes.*

Although the Spitfire pilots had a lie-in that day, normally they made an earlier start, as Flying Officer George Barclay of 249 Squadron, who was 19 in June 1940, recalled:

"*I woke as the airman orderly tapped my shoulder and repeated, 'Come along sir, come along sir, 4:30' in my ear. It was very cold in the hut and dark, so I wrestled with myself for a few minutes and then jumped out of bed and put on my flying kit quickly. Irvin trousers over my pyjamas, sweater, flying boots, scarf, Irvin jacket… I left the hut to look at my aeroplane.*
I climbed into the cockpit out of which the fitter had just stepped… I checked the instruments one by one: petrol tanks full; tail trimming wheels neutral; airscrew fine pitch; directional gyro set; helmet on; reflector sight with oxygen and R/T leads connected – in fact everything as I liked it for a quick getaway when we scrambled. **"**

"Returning to the hut I found the orderly lighting the fire by the light of a hurricane lamp, while Ginger lay fast asleep in a deck chair, his head lolling down on his yellow Mae-West. I lay down, and immediately became unconscious as if doped... What seemed the next moment I woke with a terrific start to see everyone pouring out of the hut... I could hear the telephone orderly repeating: 'Dover 26,000; fifty-plus bandits approaching from south-east.'

Percy shouted, 'Scramble, George, lazy bastard,' and automatically I ran out. Parachute on, pulled into cockpit by crew who had already started the engine. Straps, helmet, gloves, check the knobs, taxi out, get into the right position in my section and take off. I put the R/T on, and only then do I wake up and realize I am in the air flying No 2 in Yellow Section. "

Above: *The Mark IX Spitfire introduced in July 1942 had a tighter turning circle, a more powerful engine, a four-bladed propeller, two cannons and four machine guns, housed in the wings.*

Left: *The aircrews of the Battle of Britain had a unique camaraderie. They knew that few of them would survive the battle, but they had faith in their planes. They were confident that the Spitfire was superior to anything the Germans could throw at them and were determined to win whatever the cost.*

Below: *Spitfire pilots of Number 19 Squadron had few minutes to relax between sorties during the Battle of Britain. Here (left to right) Pilot Officer W. Cummingham, Sub-Lieutenant A.G. "the Admiral" Blake of the Fleet Air Arm and Flying Officer F.N. Brinsden with his spaniel enjoy the sunshine outside the crew room at Manor Farm, Fowlmere, Cambridgeshire. The following month Blake was killed in a dogfight over Chelmsford, Essex.*

Right: After the RAF bombed Berlin on 25 August 1940 – a thing Hitler had promised the German people would never happen – he instructed the Luftwaffe to blitz Britain's cities instead of bombing the airfields. This gave the RAF, by then on its last legs, a much-needed respite.

The story of a day in the life of a Spitfire pilot is taken up by Flight Lieutenant (later Air Vice Marshal) Sandy Johnstone of 602 Squadron.

"As the twelve Spitfires manoeuvred into formation, and climbed for the east, I glanced down at my watch. Under ninety seconds. 'Not bad. Hope the old man was impressed.' I started to wonder if we'd be too late again. Somehow the Controllers seemed slower these days. (They were – the communications network had been hard hit. But what they gave was far more accurate… well, sometimes. Everyone was learning.) 'Villa Leader, hullo, Villa Leader. Many bandits approaching Dungeness, Angels 15 and above.'

I had to start thinking tactics, we should really add a couple of thousand feet to our directed height, better to be a little too high than caught in the murderous fire raining down from the 109s…

Shimmering in the morning sun, wave upon wave of bombers, driving for London. Stepped above and behind, the serried ranks of Messerschmitts. Covering mile upon mile of sky, as far as the eye could see. It was at once magnificent and terrible. 'Villa Squadron, aim for the bombers. Look out for snappers coming down… here they come… Villa, break, break.'

Proctor was jinking left, then right, as the tracer flashed past; suddenly, a twin reared up in his sights – long glasshouse, a 110. He let fly, saw little chips float off as the Messerschmitt completed its bunt. One damaged. He dived for the protection of the haze."

"I was there again, and cautiously lifted the Spitfire up again, and was once again shocked by the sight of hundreds of black-crossed aircraft in unbroken phalanxes boring for London. What had all the sweat, the turmoil, the sacrifices of the last few minutes been for, I wondered. I squirted at a Heinkel, and sank below the haze as it flew solidly on. I headed east, then rose again, hoping to come on the flank of the raid. Still they were there in dozens. By now, I was quite alone, fuel was low and I circled long enough to take in the sight of bombs raining down over the docks. Fires springing up from Tilbury, a vast white splash in the Thames Estuary. Probably one of our boys, I thought. I swung for home and three 109s slanted across from the right. Instinctively, I fired at the nearest; it rolled onto its back and dived away."

Below: *In the summer of 1940, the skies over southern England were streaked with the vapour trails left by dogfights.*

Right: *A Messerschmitt Me 109E, the Spitfire's primary adversary during the Battle of Britain.*

Right: *A Messerschmitt Me 109E, the Spitfire's primary adversary during the Battle of Britain.*

> **"**I couldn't hang around to watch the results, with the other two whipping round to attack. Yellow noses – did that really mean a crack unit? – the thought was fleeting. I fired – the guns clattered briefly, then stopped. Time to go. I shoved the nose down, twisted, jinked, aileron turned, and all the time the 109s clung to my elusive Spitfire. These boys were really good. With the altimeter unwinding like a sweep second hand, I finally found sanctuary right down among the Slough balloon barrage, and threaded my way carefully to the west. **"**

From there he flew back to base at Westampnett, outside Chichester in West Sussex, with just six gallons of fuel left. But that was not the end of it. Spitfire pilots were seeing action several times a day.

Another flight officer explains the quick turnaround:

> *I landed the Spitfire back at the home base, and bumped my way across the grass towards the hangars, throwing the hood back, and filled my lungs with fresh, clean English air. I came to a standstill, and the ground staff were immediately taken to task in refuelling and rearming. I jumped out onto the wing, then down to the ground, 'Running on fumes now, are we Sir?' said the sergeant bending down and looking at me from under the wing. 'We both are,' I replied, pulling my helmet and goggles off and making my way over to the hut…*
>
> *As I got near to the dispersal hut, I saw a lean figure hurriedly put his head out of the window, 'B Flight, Scramble!' He had hardly got all the words out of his mouth as five or six bodies that were lazily lounging around outside sprang to their feet and ran to their awaiting aircraft… By the time I got inside, the place was deserted except for the dispatch clerk and Horton who had already beaten me down. 'Any of the others back?' I asked, pouring a cup of tea from the urn… The rest that we had all looked forward to was short-lived. I was just about to go and see the 'old man' when the telephone rang again, there was a short silence then 'Everybody up… scramble.' There had been hardly enough time to service the aircraft, but we ran all the same, fired up the Merlins and within seconds we were bouncing across the grass with throttles open, and doing it all over again.*

Right: *Although, in the evening light, the vapour trails looked like fireworks, a life-or-death struggle was being fought out in the airspace over London.*

An Australian flying officer takes over the action:

"With South London below, I caught a glimpse of a formation of enemy bombers as we turned southwest of London. I decided to manoeuvre our section to engage a group of Dornier 17s from the beam but at the last instant the Germans turned so that a co-ordinated assault becomes impossible. My plan had gone astray: 'Villa Squadron, Villa Squadron, okay boys… pick your target, break… break.' I instructed the men to break up and make individual attacks; I took the leading Dornier. I turned, then closed fast, I fired a four second burst before diving underneath and swinging around for a second attack from the other side. Again I fired for four seconds. The leading Dornier seemed undamaged but suddenly the second bomber in the formation broke away and fell into a dive. I turned off, and spotted a single Messerschmitt Bf 109 below and ahead. I followed it through the thick smoke billowing over the Thames and finally caught up with it over the estuary. I fired for three seconds. The 109 was hit and I closed in to 50 yards and fired for the last time. Pieces of the German fighter were torn away before it crashed into the sea…

We gained height where the air is a little clearer and had more room to move in safety as the bombers were below us and with no sign of 109s. A short conversation and I instructed them to go in again. Adams picked a target and banked away and I lost sight of him as he went down. Baker put his nose down and headed for a group of three Dorniers, I followed him to the left and behind. 'Villa break, Villa break, bandits two o'clock.' I gathered that it would only be a matter of minutes before the 109s would be on us."

"Baker was still diving down at the bombers. He was ahead of me as he closed in on a straggling Dornier. I continued to follow him down and saw him make a quarter attack on the German bomber. Large pieces flew off the enemy machine, then a wing crumpled as it went down spinning. An instant later I saw a Spitfire, which I assumed to be Baker's, spinning down with about a third of its wing broken off... Had there been a collision? The Spitfire spun wildly and he had no chance to bail out. Another casualty of this wretched war.

After doing my best to forget for the time being what I saw, I turned and attacked the bombers, evaded more 109s, I got a Dornier, and a probable, and damaged a Messerschmitt, but with ammunition exhausted, and fuel tanks close to empty, we landed back at our airfield in ones and twos..."

Each squadron was supposed to be allowed one day's rest a week, but that was not always possible. A normal day could begin as early as 3.30 am and carried on until stand down at around 8 pm. Some flights or entire squadrons would be at readiness to take off within five minutes which, in practice, meant two or three minutes. Sometimes there would be a section on standby, with the pilots in their cockpits and able to be off the ground in a minute or so. Breakfast or a sandwich lunch would be brought to the dispersal points around the airfield.

Another airman continues the tale:

"It was now just after midday, we had flown two sorties today and that had taken the stuffing out of most of us, we were glad of the rest… Sooner or later though, the action-charged instruction came through. The orderly would pause, listen and then bawl: 'Squadron scramble, Maidstone, Angels two zero.'"

"Before he'd relayed the message we were away sprinting to our Spitfires… As we ran, the fitters fired the starter cartridges and the propellers turned with engines roaring into life. From strapping in to chocks away it was just a matter of seconds. We taxied to the take-off point on the broad grass airfield and, pausing only to get the last aircraft into position, the squadron commander's upraised hand signal then came down, and I led a flotilla of twelve Spitfires that were gunning their throttles and speeding away on the take-off in a wide V formation.

As we got airborne, we snapped the canopies shut and, pulling the undercarriage lever, the wheels sucked into the wells. I glanced around on all sides, making sure that the squadron were all in position. 'Rastus Villa airborne,' I called over the R/T, to which the ground controller replied, 'OK, Villa leader, one hundred-plus bandits south of Ashford heading north-west angels fifteen. Vector 130, Buster.' Buster meant the fastest speed attainable, so there was no time for sightseeing this trip…

We struggled to gain every inch of height in the shortest possible time. We gradually emerged out of the filthy brown haze which perpetually hung like a blanket over London. Suddenly around 12,000 feet we broke through the smog layer and a different world emerged, startling in its sun-drenched clarity. Long streaming contrails snaked way above us from the Channel coast, as the Messerschmitt high-flying fighters weaved protectively over their menacing bomber formations. Our radios became almost unintelligible as pilots in our numerous intercepting squadrons called out sightings, attack orders, warnings and frustrated oaths. Somehow, a familiar voice of any one of our pilots would call out and break through the radio chatter with an urgent, 'Villa leader, bandits eleven o'clock level'."

At this point Flight-Lieutenant Al Deere takes over the action:

"I fastened on to the tail of a yellow-nosed Messerschmitt. I fought to bring my guns to bear as the range rapidly decreased and, when the wingspan of the enemy aircraft fitted snugly into the range scale bars of my reflector sight, I pressed the firing button. There was an immediate response from my eight Brownings which, to the accompaniment of a slight bucketing from my aircraft, spat a stream of lethal lead target-wards. 'Got you,' I muttered to myself as the small dancing yellow flames of exploding De Wilde bullets splattered along the Messerschmitt's fuselage. Before I could fire another burst, two 109s wheeled in behind me. I broke hard into attack, pulling the Spitfire into a climbing, spiralling turn, as I did so: a manoeuvre I had discovered in previous combats with 109s to be particularly effective. And it was no less effective now: the Messerschmitts literally 'fell out of the sky' as they stalled in an attempt to follow me.

I soon found another target. About 3,000 yards in front of me, and at the same level, a Hun was just completing a turn preparatory to re-entering the fray. He must have seen me almost immediately; he rolled out of his turn towards me so that a head-on attack became inevitable. Using both hands on the control column to steady the aircraft and to keep my aim steady, I peered through the reflector sight at the rapidly closing 109. We appeared to open fire together, and immediately a hail of lead thudded into my Spitfire. One moment, the Messerschmitt was a clearly defined shape, its wingspan nicely enclosed within the circle of my reflector sight, and the next it was on top of me, a terrifying blur which blotted out the sky ahead. Then we hit."

Left: Flying in small formations, Spitfires managed to dominate the skies of England. Their role was vital. If Britain had not remained out of Nazi hands, there would have been nowhere for the Allies to build up their forces for D-Day.

"The impact pitched me violently forward on to my cockpit harness, the straps of which bit viciously into my shoulders. At the same moment, the control column was snatched abruptly from my gripping fingers by a momentary, but powerful, reversal of elevator load. In a flash it was all over: there was clear sky ahead of me, and I thought for a moment, 'God, I'm still alive.' But smoke and flame were pouring from the engine, which began to vibrate, slowly at first, but now with increasing momentum, causing the now regained control column to jump backwards and forwards in my hand. I had to think quickly, I closed the throttle, and reached forward to flick off the ignition switches. But before I could do so, the engine seized and the airscrew came to an abrupt halt. I saw with amazement that the blades had been bent almost double with the impact of the collision, the 109 must have been just above when we hit.

Smoke poured into the cockpit, I tugged at the hood release toggle, but could not release it… There was only one thing to do, and that was to keep the aircraft under control. The speed had now dropped off considerably and with a strong backward pressure on the stick, I was able to keep a reasonable gliding altitude. Frantically, I peered through the smoke and flame that was enveloping the engine, trying to seek out what lay ahead. I daren't turn the aircraft, I had no idea as to what other damage may have been done, and at low level, even a small turn would be out of the question.

Through a miasmatic cloud of flame and smoke the ground suddenly appeared ahead of me. The next moment a post flashed by my wing tip and then the Spitfire struck the ground and ricocheted back into the air again, finally returning to earth with a jarring impact, and once again I was jerked forward on to my harness. The straps held fast, and continued to do so as the aircraft ploughed its way through a succession of posts before finally coming to rest on the edge of a cornfield. The now dense smoke blinded my eyes, and my throat felt raw; I tried to keep swallowing, but it was almost as if my tongue was being welded to the roof of my mouth. For the first time, I became frantic with fear, I tore at my harness release pin then battered at the perspex hood in an effort to escape from the cockpit which entombed me. Then at last, with a splintering crash, the hood finally cracked open, thus I was able to scramble clear from the cockpit and into the safety of the surrounding field. **"**

From there he would have to get to the nearest airfield and cadge a lift back to base. After a night down the local pub, he would be up again the next morning, ready to take to the skies again in a new Spitfire.

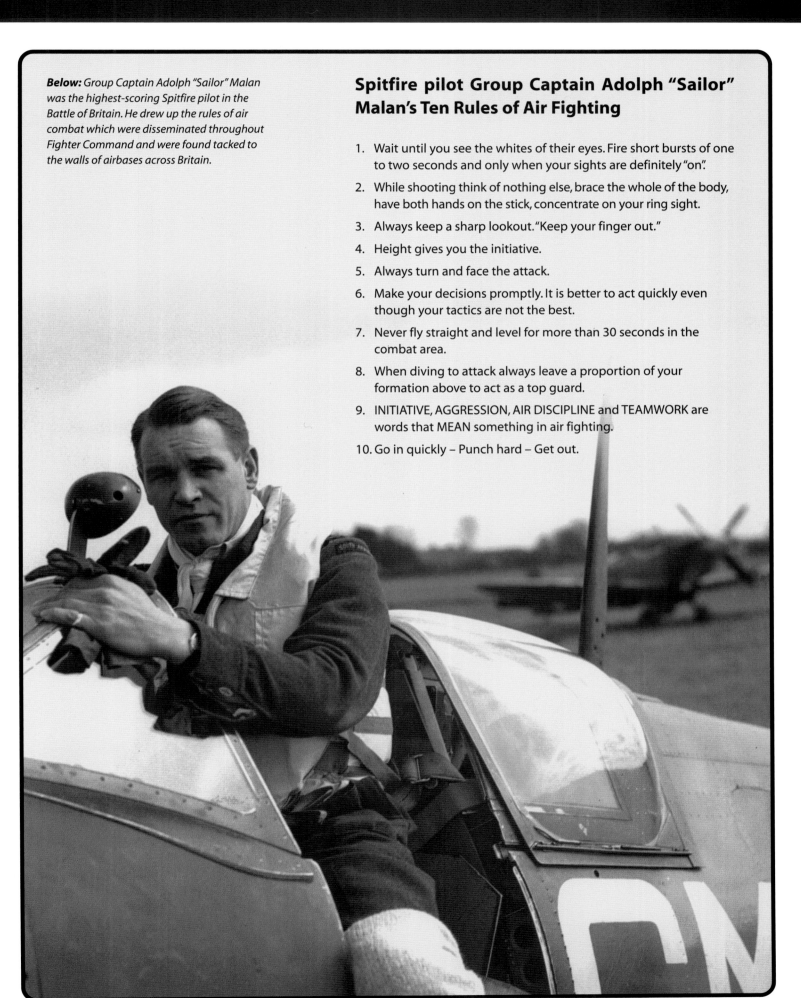

Below: Group Captain Adolph "Sailor" Malan was the highest-scoring Spitfire pilot in the Battle of Britain. He drew up the rules of air combat which were disseminated throughout Fighter Command and were found tacked to the walls of airbases across Britain.

Spitfire pilot Group Captain Adolph "Sailor" Malan's Ten Rules of Air Fighting

1. Wait until you see the whites of their eyes. Fire short bursts of one to two seconds and only when your sights are definitely "on".

2. While shooting think of nothing else, brace the whole of the body, have both hands on the stick, concentrate on your ring sight.

3. Always keep a sharp lookout. "Keep your finger out."

4. Height gives you the initiative.

5. Always turn and face the attack.

6. Make your decisions promptly. It is better to act quickly even though your tactics are not the best.

7. Never fly straight and level for more than 30 seconds in the combat area.

8. When diving to attack always leave a proportion of your formation above to act as a top guard.

9. INITIATIVE, AGGRESSION, AIR DISCIPLINE and TEAMWORK are words that MEAN something in air fighting.

10. Go in quickly – Punch hard – Get out.

Above: The wreckage of a Messerschmitt 110 fighter bomber that was brought down after a raid on Croydon in August 1940.

Training

Australian undergraduate Richard Hillary quit Oxford to join the RAF. On beginning training, he wrote: "The Spitfires stood in two lines outside 'A' Flight pilots' room. The dull grey-brown of the camouflage could not conceal the clear-cut beauty, the wicked simplicity of their lines. I hooked up my parachute and climbed awkwardly into the low cockpit. I noticed how small my field of vision was … With one or two very sharp movements on the stick I blacked myself out for a few seconds, but the machine was sweeter to handle than any other that I had flown. I put it through every manoeuvre that I knew of and it responded beautifully. I ended with two flick rolls and turned back for home… I could fly a Spitfire… It remained to be seen whether I could fight in one."

Above: The Battle of Britain spawned a slew of memoirs. The first came from Richard Hillary, author of The Last Enemy, published in 1942. He was killed the following year.

In Combat

Richard Hillary was assigned to 603 Squadron in Aberdeen on 6 July 1940. On 10 August, 603 Squadron was ordered south to Hornchurch. Over the next three weeks he fought valiantly. Then on 3 September 1940, he had made his fifth "kill" when he was shot down by a Messerschmitt Bf 109. Recalling the incident he wrote: "When we did first sight them, nobody shouted, as I think we all saw them at the same moment. They must have been 500 to 1,000 feet above us and coming straight on like a swarm of locusts. The next moment we were in among them and it was each man for himself. As soon as they saw us they spread out and dived, and the next ten minutes were a blur of twisting machines and tracer bullets. One Messerschmitt went down in a sheet of flame on my right, and a Spitfire hurtled past in a half-roll; I was weaving and turning in a desperate attempt to gain height, with the machine practically hanging on the airscrew…

"Then, just below me and to my left, I saw what I had been praying for – a Messerschmitt climbing and away from the sun. I closed in to 200 yards, and from slightly to one side gave him a two-second burst: fabric ripped off the wing and black smoke poured from the engine, but he did not go down. Like a fool, I did not break away, but put in another three-second burst. Red flames shot upwards and he spiralled out of sight. At that moment, I felt a terrific explosion which knocked the control stick from my hand, and the whole machine quivered like a stricken animal. In a second, the cockpit was a mass of flames: instinctively, I reached up to open the hood. It would not move… I remember thinking 'So this is it!' and putting both hands to my eyes. Then I passed out."

He awoke in the sea, was rescued and taken to East Grinstead where reconstructive plastic surgery was being pioneered. His hands and face were rebuilt, though he was killed in an air crash shortly after returning to service in 1943.

Below: The officers of Number 92 Squadron gather in front of a Mark I Spitfire at Manston in Kent to commemorate the 130th confirmed shootdown.

Chapter 2
The Redoubtable Mr Mitchell

The genius behind the Spitfire was the self-effacing Reginald Joseph Mitchell. He was born on 20 May 1895 in the small village of Butt Lane near Newcastle-under-Lyme in the Potteries area of England. His parents were both teachers. At school he showed a flair for both mathematics and art, but his first love was engineering. In 1911 he was apprenticed to a firm of locomotive makers in nearby Stoke-on-Trent. He graduated to the drawing office and, as part of his apprenticeship, studied mathematics and engineering at night school. In 1917, after completing his apprenticeship, he applied for a job as assistant to Hubert Scott-Paine, the owner and chief designer of the Supermarine Aviation Works in the Woolston district of Southampton. He was offered the position and sent for his belongings rather than travelling back to the Midlands.

Above: *The designer Reginald Joseph Mitchell did not live to see the Spitfire's "finest hour", but he did live long enough to see his famous creation take to the air on its first test flights.* ***Opposite:*** *Mitchell's birthplace.*

REGINALD·J·MITCHELL·C.B.E
A.M.I.C.E.   F.R.Ae.S.
DESIGNER OF THE SPITFIRE
WAS BORN HERE
20th MAY 1895

Newcastle-under-Lyme Civic Society

Reginald Mitchell
1895 - 1937
designer of the Spitfire aeroplane
was born here

Rotary Club of Kidsgrove

BOROUGH OF NEWCASTLE UNDER LYME

BUTT LANE

He was followed by Florence Dayson, headmistress of the Dresden Infants' School back in the Potteries. Although she was some 11 years older than him, she gave up her job and married a man who was only just out of his apprenticeship.

Mitchell impressed his new bosses. Within a year he had been promoted to assistant works manager. In 1919, he took over as chief designer and in 1920 he became chief engineer. He was just 25. Between 1920 and 1936 he designed 24 different aircraft ranging from light aircraft and fighters to huge flying boats and bombers. This prodigious output set him apart from other aircraft designers. One of Mitchell's talents was his ability to develop an aircraft to a certain point, then hand responsibility to others. By 1923, Mitchell was indispensable to Supermarine, who gave him a ten-year contract. In 1927, he was appointed technical director.

Below: *R.J. Mitchell and the team at Supermarine greet King George VI when he came to inspect the one and only Supermarine Swan.*

Supermarine had always specialized in flying boats. Mitchell developed a series – the Sea Eagle, the Scarab and the Swan. Only one Swan was built and, although it went into service carrying passengers between England and France, it was essentially a prototype for the Southampton, a military flying boat. Due to the success of the Swan, the Air Ministry took the unusual step of buying six Southamptons direct from the drawing board. They went into service in 1925 and were sold to a number of other countries. Six RAF squadrons were equipped with the Southampton. Eighty-three went into service and remained in service until 1936.

Supermarine Southampton

In the early 1920s, Mitchell designed the Supermarine Swan, an experimental wooden twin-engined biplane amphibian aircraft, as a replacement for the RAF's Felixstowe F5s. First flown on 25 March 1924, the Swan was powered by two 350-horsepower Rolls-Royce Eagle IX engines. It was later re-engined with two 450-horsepower Napier Lion engines. In 1926, after it had been evaluated at the Marine Aircraft Experimental Establishment, it was loaned to Imperial Airways. With a capacity of ten, it provided a passenger service between England and France until it was scrapped in 1927.

Due to the success of the Swan, the Air Ministry ordered six Southamptons direct from the drawing board, considering the Swan effectively the prototype. The first flight of a production aircraft was made on 10 March 1925, and it was delivered later that year. Eight were sold to Argentina. Turkey bought six aircraft and Australia bought two from the RAF. Japan also purchased one that was later converted into an 18-passenger airliner. Another was modified for civilian use and operated by Imperial Airways.

The Southampton was a two-engine biplane flying boat, with the engines mounted between the wings. The Mark I had both its hull and its wings manufactured from wood; the Mark II had a metal hull. This change gave a weight saving of 900 lb and increased the range by approximately 200 miles. In 1929, 24 of the Mark Is were converted by replacing the wooden hulls with metal ones. Some of the later aircraft were built with metal wings and designated the Mark III. The military versions had three positions for machine guns, one in the nose and two staggered in the rear fuselage.

Right: *The Supermarine Swan takes to the air. It carried passengers between England and France, and was the prototype for the Southampton military flying boat.*

When Supermarine was taken over by Vickers-Armstrong in 1928 it was written into the contract that Mitchell must stay with the company for at least five years, such was his reputation. At first Vickers tried to get Mitchell to co-operate with their own top designer – Barnes Wallis, the man responsible for the Wellington bomber and the bouncing bomb used on the famous "Dambusters" raid. But Mitchell was his own man and would walk out of the room when Barnes Wallis walked in. Vickers soon relented and let the Supermarine design team carry on independently as before.

In Mitchell's hands, Supermarine was one of the few British aircraft companies that remained profitable during the Great Depression that followed the stock-market crash of 1929. It did this despite employing a higher proportion of skilled men than their competitors. The manufacture of the Southampton and the Stranraer flying boat, which went into service with the RAF in 1937, kept Supermarine afloat while other companies were failing.

Supermarine Stranraer

The Stranraer was designed by Mitchell to fulfil Air Ministry Specification R.24/31 for a coastal reconnaissance flying boat for the RAF. It was initially rejected, but Supermarine proceeded with the type as a private venture, first known as the Southampton V. A contract was placed in 1933 for a prototype powered by two 820-horsepower Bristol Pegasus IIIM engines and the type became known as the Stranraer. The structure was mainly made in aluminium, with the hull covered with sheet metal and the wings with fabric.

The prototype was delivered in 1934. The following year, an initial order was placed for 17 aircraft. The production version was fitted with the 920-horsepower Pegasus X engine. It went into service in April 1937. A total of 40 Stranraers were built by Supermarine and in Canada by Canadian Vickers Ltd, another subsidiary of Vickers-Armstrong. The last Stranraer was delivered in April 1939. During World War II they were used for anti-submarine and convoy escort patrols. The Stranraer was withdrawn from operational service by the RAF in March 1941 but continued to be used for training until October 1942. They continued in service with the Royal Canadian Air Force until 1945. Some passed into civilian use in British Columbia after the war.

In service, the Stranraer was sometimes derisively referred to as the "whistling sh*thouse". This was because the toilet opened out directly to the air and when the seat was lifted, the airflow caused the lavatory to whistle.

Left: *The Supermarine Stranraer was developed privately by the company, showing a commitment to aeronautical development that would pay dividends with the Spitfire.*

Left: *The Supermarine Sea Lion entered for the Schneider Trophy in 1919. The race was abandoned due to fog and the Sea Lion sank.*

Despite the success of Supermarine's flying boats, Mitchell is more commonly associated with the design of high-speed aircraft for the Schneider Trophy races between 1922 and 1931. Mitchell's first winner was the Sea Lion II, a small biplane flying boat that won in Naples in 1922 with an average speed of 145.7 miles per hour. The following year, at Cowes, the trophy was won by the American Curtiss CR-3, designed by Glenn Curtiss. The plane's Curtiss D-12 engine was the inspiration for the Rolls-Royce Merlin, which would eventually power the Spitfire.

Right: *The Supermarine Sea Lion Mark V near the company's factory at Itchen.*

Glenn Curtiss

Born in 1878 in Hammondsport, New York, Glenn Curtiss began his career building engines for bicycles. His lightweight designs were much in demand by the pioneers of powered flight. In 1904, he built an engine for the dirigible "California Arrow". In 1908, he won the Scientific American trophy for the first flight of over one kilometre – America's first officially recognized heavier-than-air flight. This involved him in a series of lawsuits over patents with the Wright Brothers that he lost in 1913. Further lawsuits were dropped during World War I and were resolved when they joined forces to form the Curtiss-Wright Corporation.

Curtiss was the first builder of seaplanes, which first took to the air in 1911. After showing how his designs could be used in conjunction with warships, he won a contract to produce seaplanes for the US Navy, supplying them to Britain and Russia during World War I. His most famous design was the JN-4, or Jenny, which was used as a wartime trainer. After the war it became a favourite of barnstormers and made the first Canadian mail flight over the Rocky Mountains.

His Curtiss CR-3 won the Schneider Trophy in two consecutive races in 1923 and 1925, along with the 1925 Pulitzer Trophy with a top speed of 232.573 miles per hour. He died in Buffalo, New York, in 1930.

Right: *The Curtiss Racer that topped 233 miles per hour.*

Left: *American aircraft pioneer Glenn Curtiss, whose Curtiss D-12 engine provided the inspiration for the Rolls-Royce Merlin that would power the Spitfire.*

After seeing the CR-3 seaplane, Mitchell abandoned his flying boat design, where the bottom of the fuselage acts a hull, and began developing a series of streamlined seaplanes which stood proud of the water on floats. The first S4 – S for Schneider – side-slipped from a jetty at Bay Shore Park in Baltimore during the trials before the 1925 Schneider Trophy and was wrecked.

Above: *In 1925, Mitchell abandoned flying boats and began designing floatplanes. With the S4, here, it is possible to see the shape of the Spitfire beginning to evolve.*

Above: *The S5, with a Napier engine, would regain the Schneider Trophy for Supermarine.*

But the S5 recaptured the Trophy for Supermarine in 1927. The S6, with a new Rolls-Royce engine, retained it in 1929, while the S6B won again in 1931, averaging 340 miles per hour around the course above the Solent. The S6B aircraft went on to break the air-speed record twice. It was the first aircraft to top 400 miles per hour, with a new world record of 407.5 miles per hour. Mitchell was awarded the CBE in 1932 for his contribution to high-speed flight.

Below: *The Napier Lion Series VIIB engine that powered the S5 to first place in 1927.*

Above: *The Schneider Trophy-winning Supermarine S5.*

Below: The Supermarine S6A number N247, with a Rolls-Royce engine, that won the Schneider Trophy in 1929, clocking a speed of 328.6 miles per hour.

Above: *The Supermarine S6B number S1595 that won the Schneider Trophy in 1931. It is now on display in the Science Museum in London.*

Below: *Supermarine's Schneider Trophy-winning team at the Solent in 1931. This time they topped 340 miles per hour, though the S6B would go on to take the world record at 407.5 miles per hour.*

Above: The winning S6B at Calshot Castle on the Solent with the Supermarine team – RAF pilots Waghorn and Atcherley in the front row, and Stainforth, Orlebar and Moon behind. Mitchell, with characteristic modesty, is at the back to the right.

The Schneider Trophy

Officially the Coupe d'Aviation Maritime Jacques Schneider, this was a prize competition for seaplanes, established in 1911 by French financier, balloonist and aircraft enthusiast Jacques Schneider. Along with the cup, it offered a prize of 25,000 gold francs, worth roughly £1,000 back then. Held 11 times between 1913 and 1931 – first in Monaco, then in the home waters of the previous year's winner – it was meant to encourage technical advances in civil aviation, but became a contest for pure speed. The winner was the fastest plane over a triangular course initially of 280 kilometres, later of 350 kilometres. The races were very popular and some attracted crowds of over 200,000 spectators. Under the rules of the Fédération Aéronautique Internationale, any competitor who won the cup three times in five years retained it – a feat achieved by Supermarine and R.J. Mitchell in 1931 – and the competition was at an end.

Right: *Flight Lieutenant John Boothman, the winning pilot in the 1931 race.*

Left: *The Schneider Trophy – after winning it 4 times, under the rules Supermarine got to keep it. The competition was then at an end.*

Left: *The winner of the Schneider Trophy got to host the following year's race. A win by Mario de Bernadi of Italy, at Hampton Roads in the US in 1926, meant that the 1927 race took place in Venice.*

The design lessons learned from Mitchell's Schneider Trophy winners were hard to apply to civil aviation which, in any case, was suffering a cutback due to the Depression. But because of the success of the Southampton, Supermarine were well placed to produce tenders and designs for the Air Ministry, who were on the look-out for high-speed planes – Mitchell's forté.

In 1930 the Air Ministry issued Specification F7/30 that called for a new fighter armed with four machine guns. In response, Mitchell designed the Supermarine Type 224, which eventually lost out to the Gloster Gladiator. However, Mitchell had learnt some important lessons in the Type 224's design and decided to have another go. Even before the Type 224 was rejected, he had begun work on the Type 300, which would eventually become the Spitfire. However, his health was already failing.

During a routine medical check-up, Mitchell was diagnosed with cancer of the rectum and in August 1933 he had a colostomy. In the 1930s, this operation, with its unpleasant consequences, normally left those who survived debilitated. Mitchell could have retired at this point, or simply arranged to work from home. Instead, he went back to work. Not only that, in December 1933 he started flying lessons, earning his pilot's licence in July 1934. By this time the Type 224 had already taken to the air and, four months later, the prototype Spitfire would be on the drawing board.

Below: *The Supermarine Walrus, designed by R.J. Mitchell in 1935, found a role in air-sea rescue during World War II.*

Supermarine Walrus

The Supermarine Walrus was a marine reconnaissance biplane. Powered by a single Bristol Pegasus VI radial engine, it was the first amphibious aircraft to be launched by catapult with a full military load. Its wings could be folded, giving a stowage width of 17 feet 11 inches on ship. Unusually its control column could be unplugged and passed between the pilot and co-pilot.

Strengthened for catapult-launching, it could be looped and bunted, though water from the bilges would soak the pilots. Armed with two Vickers K machine guns in the nose and rear fuselage, it could carry 760 lb of bombs or depth charges beneath the lower wings.

The RAAF (Royal Australian Air Force) ordered 24 of the prototype Seagull V from the drawing board in 1935, while the RAF took the first production Walrus, taking to the air 16 March 1936. There were three major variants: the metal-hulled Seagull V and Walrus I, and the wooden-hulled Walrus II. In all, 740 were built. Dubbed the "Shagbat" or "Steam-pigeon" due to steam produced when water struck the engine, it saw service with the RAF, Fleet Air Arm, RAAF, RNZN, RCAF, and RNZAF.

Below: *Although it was heavy and cumbersome, the Supermarine Walrus could be launched by catapult from a ship. To return, it would land alongside, then be winched back on board.*

Another of Mitchell's outstanding designs was the Supermarine Walrus amphibian. Introduced in 1935, it was used throughout World War II in an air-sea rescue role. He also designed the Supermarine Air Yacht, designed to carry wealthy patrons on airborne cruises around the Mediterranean. But perhaps one of the best of Mitchell's designs was never made. It was the Supermarine Bomber which, had it become airborne, would have out-performed any other bomber in the first five years of World War II.

Supermarine Bomber

In designing the Spitfire Mitchell had pioneered a unique method of wing construction, the single spar with a thick metal leading edge. Filling this leading edge section with fuel would produce an aircraft with a very thin wing and slim aerodynamic fuselage while still having a large fuel capacity. This was the key concept for Mitchell's Project B12/36, the Supermarine Bomber. Mitchell's design would have carried a bomb-load almost as great as the Lancaster at greater heights and at a speed close to that of the Spitfire. It would have given the RAF a bomber superior to every other deployed in World War II except the Boeing B-29 Superfortress, which was not introduced until May 1944. As it was, Supermarine did not have the factory space or the workforce to move the project forward and, when the prototype was destroyed on its jigs in a Luftwaffe raid on the Supermarine factory in Woolston in September 1940, the bomber project was cancelled. Air Ministry Specification B12/36 was fulfilled by the Short Stirling Bomber.

Left: *With Mitchell's super-bomber out of the running, the Air Ministry contract was won by the Short Stirling Bomber.*

Mitchell was an idiosyncratic man. Around people he appeared shy and a slight stammer caused him real distress when he was called upon to give speeches, although at Supermarine and with people he knew, he was aware of his own ability and supremely confident. An able manager, he was a very good listener – even the most junior draughtsman would be allowed to have their say in the complex job of designing aircraft. However, he would always take full responsibility for a project, never letting his staff be criticized by anyone other than himself. When he hit a problem, he would take a long time thinking it over – the people he worked with learned not to interrupt him while he was thinking. But when he came up with a solution, he would be galvanized into action.

Mitchell was particularly conscious about safety, which was not always a consideration in the early days of powered flight. During the same era, cutting-edge designers such as Messerschmitt regularly lost test pilots. True, there were some inherent dangers in his designs. The Supermarine S4 developed a dangerous wing flutter, but this would have been impossible to predict with the design tools available then. The original Supermarine Air Yacht was underpowered and the Type 224 had no flaps. This meant it had to land at high speed, which would have been particularly dangerous at night – a fault he corrected in the final design. Mitchell was one of the few aircraft designers of his day who actually learned to fly, albeit late in his life.

Right: A rare picture of R.J. Mitchell alongside the prototype Spitfire K5054 at Eastleigh airfield, taken by his son Gordon on a Kodak Box Brownie.

Although Mitchell was dedicated to his work and would work late at the office, he also enjoyed a full family life with his wife Florence and his son Gordon. He enjoyed tennis, golf, snooker, shooting and sailing. He kept his boat moored at the factory slipway and would often disappear for a couple of hours' sailing in the Solent during the working day.

In 1936 Mitchell was again diagnosed with cancer. In February 1937 he went into hospital in London, but nothing could be done, and he returned to his home soon after. He was then forced to give up work, though he was often seen sitting in his car at Eastleigh airfield watching the testing of the prototype Spitfire when he should have been at home resting. In late April 1937, he flew to Vienna for treatment, but returned to England at the end of May. For the last weeks of his life, he enjoyed sitting in his garden, listening to the birds and admiring the flowers. Reginald Mitchell died of cancer on 11 June 1937 at the tragically young age of 42. Responsibility for the development of the Spitfire had already fallen to Joseph "Joe" Smith, who had served as Supermarine's chief draughtsman for many years.

While the Spitfire would be Mitchell's greatest legacy, during his last years he spent more time working on the Supermarine B12/36 bomber, the R1/36 fast anti-submarine flying boat – a specification fulfilled by the Saunders-Roe A.36 Lerwick – and the F37/35 four-cannon fighter – fulfilled by the Westland Whirlwind.

Below: A visit by the Sea Lords to the Vickers-Armstrong Supermarine works at Hursley Park, Winchester, in 1952. The Spitfire had done its work by then and its useful life was almost over.

Mitchell on Film

In 1986 Mitchell's son Gordon wrote a biography of his father called *R.J. Mitchell: Schooldays to Spitfire*. But Mitchell is perhaps better known from the biopic *The First of the Few*, directed by Leslie Howard. It also starred Leslie Howard as Mitchell and David Niven playing his test pilot. A propaganda film, it opened in 1942. The opening sequence takes on an RAF station during the Battle of Britain using pilots who fought in the battle. The film traces the story of Mitchell from his winning of the Schneider Trophy in 1922, through the design of the Spitfire, up to Mitchell's death and beyond with the Battle of Britain.

The film takes considerable dramatic licence. In one scene Mitchell and his test pilot visit Germany in the early 1930s. However, Vickers Supermarine test pilot, and the pilot of the prototype Spitfire, Captain Joe "Mutt" Summers, and the company's aerodynamicist Beverly Shenstone both visited Germany, and Mitchell's wife Florence went on a skiing holiday in Austria in the mid 1930s. However, in the film, Mitchell meets Messerschmitt in a German inn and comes away convinced he must design a fighter to protect Britain. This is total invention. The film also implies that Mitchell worked himself to death perfecting the Spitfire. In fact, he was terminally ill and spent more time on other projects. The film ends memorably with Niven, now in the RAF, fresh from a dog-fight with Messerschmitts, pushing back the cockpit canopy of his Spitfire and shouting at the sky: "They can't take the Spitfires, Mitch! They can't take them!" This is stirring stuff, but it was filmed just two years after the Spitfire had proved itself in the Battle of Britain and the war had yet to be won.

Far Left: A fictionalized scene from the film The First of the Few, *where designer R.J. Mitchell (played by Leslie Howard) visits Germany and is confronted with the Nazi menace that he would go on to thwart.*

Left: R.J. Mitchell's life was cut short by cancer and he had no time to write his memoirs. The job was done for him by his son Gordon.

Above: *The Supermarine factory at Woolston after being bombed in September 1940. As the home of the Spitfire, it was a prime target.*

Above: *Although the German bombers did considerable damage to the factories in Woolston and Itchen and killed a number of experienced aircraft workers, production had already been dispersed to ensure that there would be no shortage of Spitfires in the skies.*

Chapter 3

Vickers-Armstrong

The Spitfire was made by Vickers-Armstrong, an engineering and armaments company formed by the merger of Vickers Limited and Armstrong Whitworth in 1927. It acquired Supermarine and Mitchell's design team in 1928. Although Supermarine continued to design and build aircraft under its own name, it did not have the factory space to build Spitfires in the numbers required. Production was dispersed, which was as well. The Germans were well aware of the Spitfire's importance in the defence of Britain and in August and September 1940 – during the Battle of Britain itself – made a concerted effort to bomb Supermarine's factories in Woolston and nearby Itchen. On 26 September, they succeeded in wrecking both factories, killing 92 people and injuring many more.

Most of the casualties were experienced aircraft production workers. But production continued in other Vickers-Armstrong factories.

Vickers was begun in 1828 as a steel foundry in Sheffield owned by the miller Edward Vickers and his father-in-law George Naylor. It made steel castings and became famous for casting church bells. Edward Vickers' investments in the railways allowed him to gain control of the company. In 1854 Vickers' sons joined the company and, in 1867, Vickers, Sons & Company went public.

Above: *The US Army on manoeuvres in Texas in 1911 with a Maxim gun, one of the products of the company that would one day take over Supermarine.*

Below: *The assembly line at the Vickers, Sons & Maxim gun factory.*

In 1868 Vickers began to manufacture marine shafts and in 1872 it began casting marine propellers. Vickers produced their first armour plate in 1888 and their first artillery piece in 1890. It bought out the Barrow-in-Furness shipbuilder The Barrow Shipbuilding Company in 1897, and began fitting out ships with armour plating and ordnance. Vickers also merged with Maxim Nordenfelt Guns and Ammunitions Company to become Vickers, Sons & Maxim.

The updated design of the Maxim gun became the Vickers machine gun. It was the standard machine gun of the British Empire and was in use with the British Army for 50 years. The Royal Navy used a larger-calibre version and variants of the Vickers machine gun were used on both sides during World War I.

Below: *The Vickers, Sons & Maxim armour-plating shop.*

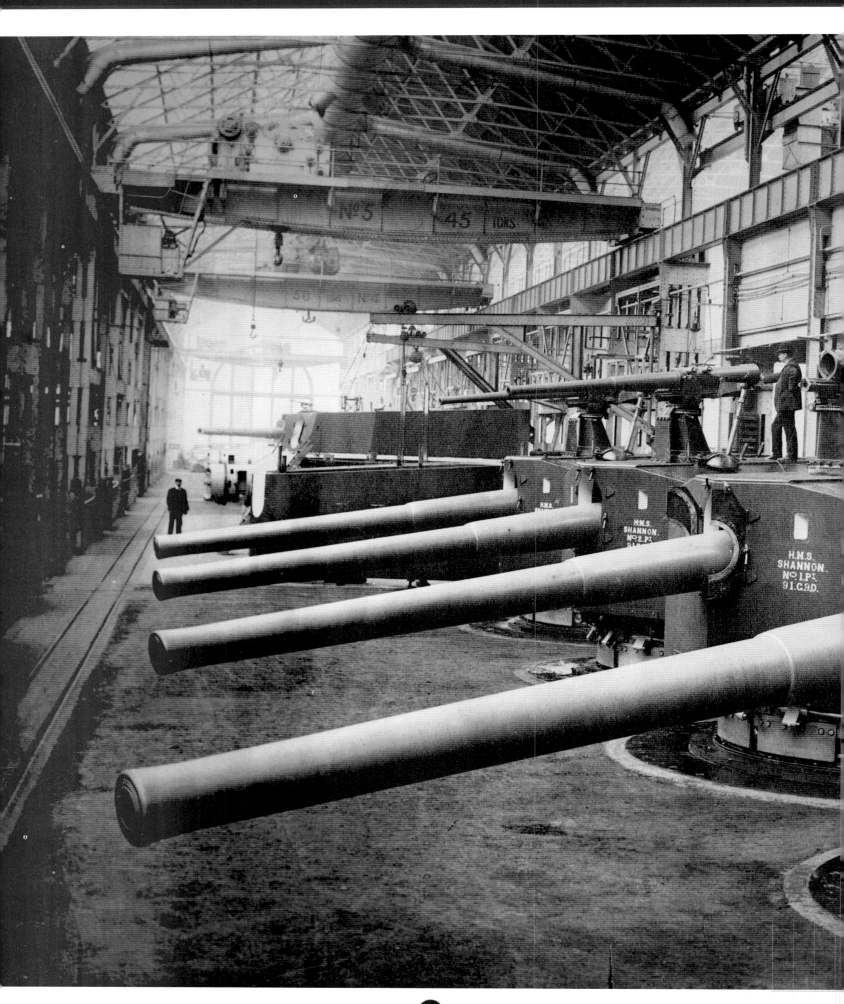

PIT Nº 6

H.M.S.
SHANNON.
Nº1.Sᵀᴰ
9 I.C.9.D.

Left: The Vickers works at Barrow-in-Furness where the company built large guns for the Royal Navy.

Above: The airship R100, built by a subsidiary of Vickers. Its sister ship, the R101, crashed on its maiden voyage in 1930, killing 48.

Left: *The Vickers machine gun was again in demand in World War I.*

In 1901 the Royal Navy's first submarine, Holland 1, was launched at the Naval Construction Yard. The company moved into car building by taking over the motor works of the Wolseley Sheep-Shearing Machine Company in 1905, which became the Wolseley Tool and Motor Car Company. In 1909 Vickers moved into airship production, abandoning rigid airships for non-rigid blimps. However, a subsidiary company made the R100, a rival to the ill-fated government-built R101. While the R100 made a successful trans-Atlantic voyage to Canada in July 1930, returning safely in August, the R101 crashed in France on her maiden flight to India, killing 48 people, on 5 October 1930, and the Air Ministry stopped further flights. The R100 was scrapped in November 1931 and its flattened framework sold for just £600.

In 1911 Vickers took a controlling interest in Whitehead and Company, the torpedo manufacturers. That same year, the company changed its name to Vickers Limited and moved into aircraft manufacture by the formation of Vickers Ltd (Aviation Department). It produced one of the first aircraft designed to carry a machine gun, the FB5 (Fighting Biplane) Gun Bus.

Right: *Three Vickers Valentias of Number 70 Squadron RAF during a flight from Hinaidi to Amadiyah in northern Iraq in 1936.*

Above: *A Vickers FB5 Gun Bus – the "fighting biplane" – was first produced in 1911.*

Left: RAF Vickers Vimys of Number 216 Squadron, based at Heliopolis in Egypt in 1925–26, fly over the race course there.

During World War I it produced the Valentia and Viking flying boats and the Vimy heavy bomber. A converted Vimy bomber became the first aircraft to cross the Atlantic non-stop. Further developed as the Virginia, it became one of the main armaments of the RAF during the inter-war years. Vickers Aviation also pioneered airliners, beginning with converted Vimy bombers.

In 1919 Vickers took over British Westinghouse electrical company and acquired Metropolitan's railway interests. However, Wolseley had been sold to the Nuffield Organisation before the merger with Armstrong Whitworth in 1927. Vickers' main business continued to be in armaments and the company produced numerous firearms. The British version of the Remington's semi-automatic M1903 Springfield rifle, designed by Jon Pedersen, was made by Vickers and, in Britain, was known as the Vickers Rifle.

Left: A Vickers Vernon, normally used as a troop transport, armed and ready for action.

Above: Vickers light tank in action in Egypt in 1940.

In the interwar period Vickers worked on several tank designs. Medium Mark I and Mark II were adopted by the British Army. The Vickers 6-ton tank was the most successful and was exported or built by other nations under licence. The Vickers A1E1 Independent tank design was never put into production, but was credited with influencing development in other nations. During World War II Vickers built large guns and tanks.

Its merger with WG Armstrong Whitworth & Company had strengthened Vickers' interests in armaments.

Left: The naval gun shop at the Armstrong works.

The Armstrong wing of the firm began in 1847, when engineer William George Armstrong founded the Elswick works at Newcastle, to produce hydraulic machinery, cranes and bridges. During the Crimean War, Armstrong developed the breech-loading gun, which was used by the re-equipped British Army. He also sold artillery to both sides during the American Civil War. In 1867 Armstrong began working with the Tyneside shipbuilding firm of Charles Mitchell, building and arming warships. In 1882, they merged to form Sir W.G. Armstrong Mitchell & Company, and equipped the Japanese fleet that defeated the Russians during the Russo-Japanese War of 1904–5.

Below: The Armstrong gun works in Newcastle-upon-Tyne, circa 1915.

In 1894 Armstrong's Elswick works built and installed the steam-driven pumping engines and hydraulic accumulator mechanism that operates London's Tower Bridge.

Armstrong Mitchell merged again with the engineering firm of Joseph Whitworth to form WG Armstrong Whitworth & Company in 1897. By that time Whitworth was dead. In his youth, precision toolmaker Joseph Whitworth had helped build Charles Babbage's computing machine, the Difference Engine. He set up on his own in 1830. In 1841, Whitworth's 55 degree angle for a screw thread became the British Standard and, at the Great Exhibition of 1851, he showed precision instruments that were accurate to one-millionth of an inch.

Below: *Armstrong Mitchell & Company equipped the Japanese fleet that defeated the Russians during the Russo-Japanese War of 1904–5.*

Below: A Whitworth gun on the wharf at Richmond, Virginia, awaiting shipment.

Whitworth then went into the business of making rifles. Though his guns were rejected by the British, they were adopted by the French Army and were taken up by Confederate snipers in the American Civil War where they were known as "Whitworth Sharpshooters". When Queen Victoria opened the first meeting of the British Rifle Association at Wimbledon in 1860, she fired a Whitworth rifle from a fixed mechanical rest, scoring a bull's eye at 400 yards.

Like Armstrong, Whitworth produced breech-loading artillery. The British Army preferred Armstrong's guns, but Whitworth found a ready market in America during the Civil War. After his death in 1887, the company merged with Armstrong.

Armstrong Whitworth expanded into the manufacture of cars and trucks in 1902, and created an "aerial department" in 1913, which became the Armstrong Whitworth Aircraft subsidiary in 1920. Meanwhile, the company continued to expand through acquisition until it merged with Vickers in 1927. The company then acquired Supermarine the following year. Pioneer aviator Noel Pemberton Billing had set up the company, Pemberton-Billing Ltd, in 1913 to produce sea-going aircraft. It also produced a couple of prototypes to shoot down Zeppelins using round-winged quadruplane designs, the Supermarine PB25 and the Supermarine Nighthawk.

Left: *Two 80-pounder Whitworth guns on Morris Island, South Carolina. The naval battery there was used to bombard Fort Sumter, starting the American Civil War.*

Noel Pemberton Billing

The *Dictionary of National Biography* describes Supermarine's founder Noel Pemberton Billing as "aviator and self-publicist". Born in Hampstead in 1881, he stowed away on a ship bound for Mozambique at the age of 13. After trying his hand at a number of menial jobs, he joined the Natal Mounted Police and, after fighting in the Boer War, was invalided out. Returning to England, he was quick to see the military significance of aviation. From 1908 to 1910, he edited the journal *Aerocraft*, and designed and tested three monoplanes from his own airstrip in Fambridge, Essex. After making money in yacht-broking, land speculation and writing, by 1913 he had enough money to set up his own yard on Southampton Water to build flying boats – or "supermarines".

He earned his pilot's licence after only four hours and two minutes in the air. With the outbreak of World War I, he joined the Royal Naval Air Service and organized the air-raid on the Zeppelin sheds at Friedrichshafen in November 1914. He quit in 1916 to complain about the way the air war was being handled and was elected to parliament on his second attempt. While campaigning for bombing raids on German cities, he ran the journal *Imperialist*, which claimed that the Germans were blackmailing 47,000 Britons to "propagate evils which all decent men thought had perished in Sodom and Lesbia", even naming the prime minister's wife Margot Asquith as a leading sapphist. His journal, then renamed *Vigilante*, published an article called "The Cult of the Clitoris", which implied that the actress Maud Allan, who was appearing in a private production of Salome, was a lesbian associate of the conspirators. This led to a sensational libel case, where Billing represented himself and won. Lord Alfred Douglas, a former lover of Oscar Wilde, testified in Billing's favour. Billing further annoyed the establishment by running his own "purity party" candidates at by-elections, though he himself was forced to retire from politics due to ill-heath in 1921.

The PB31E Nighthawk was developed by Noel Pemberton Billing, but it only took to the air in February 1917 after the company had become Supermarine Aviation Works Ltd. It was a prototype anti-Zeppelin fighter with a crew of two pilots and three guns. It had two tailplanes with twin fins and rudders, one above the other, and four wings, with the six-bay fuselage mounted in the gap between the second and third wings. The cockpit was enclosed and heated.

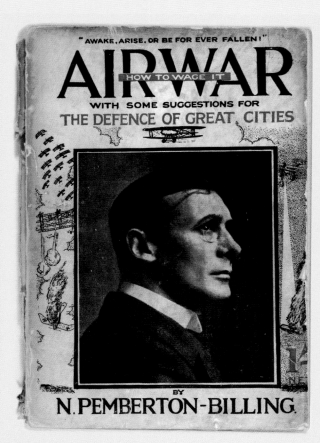

" AWAKE, ARISE, OR BE FOR EVER FALLEN!"

AIRWAR

HOW TO WAGE IT

WITH SOME SUGGESTIONS FOR
THE DEFENCE OF GREAT CITIES

BY
N. PEMBERTON-BILLING.

Left: *The founder of Supermarine, Noel Pemberton Billing, foresaw with frightening clarity the future of air war.*

It was armed with two .303-inch Lewis guns and a two-pounder (40 mm) recoilless Davis gun mounted above the top wing with 20 shells. Its trainable nose-mounted searchlight was powered by an independent petrol engine-driven generator, thought to be the first use of an airborne auxiliary power unit. Supermarine claimed that it had a top speed of 75 miles per hour, but the prototype only reached 60 miles per hour at 6,500 feet and took an hour to climb to 10,000 feet, making it totally inadequate for intercepting Zeppelins. Its Anzani engine had a reputation for unreliability and overheating, and it is unlikely that the plane would have managed the advertised endurance of 9 to 18 hours.

In 1927, he wrote a play, *High Treason*, inspired by Fritz Lang's film *Metropolis*, which was performed at the Strand Theatre. He filmed this the following year in two versions – one silent and the other an early talkie – but neither was successful. He claimed to have taken out 500 patents on devices as varied as a miniature camera for the use of spies, an unbreakable record, a two-sided stove and a gramophone. He died in 1948.

Left: *Noel Pemberton Billing was a pioneer of flight. Here he is at the controls of a Farman aeroplane, powered by a 50-horsepower Gnome engine.*

When Pemberton Billing was elected to parliament in 1916, he sold the company to his factory manager and long-time associate Hubert Scott-Paine who renamed the company Supermarine Aviation. This was the company that R.J. Mitchell joined in 1917.

Hugh Scott-Paine

The man who first employed Spitfire designer R.J. Mitchell at Supermarine, Hugh Scott-Paine, was also an aircraft and power-boat designer. Born plain Hubert Paine in Shoreham in 1891, he played truant from school to tinker with motors and spend time at Shoreham aerodrome. He later hyphenated his parents' names to get Scott-Paine. When he was 18, he met Noel Pemberton Billing and became Billing's assistant in his yacht-broking business. In 1913, when Billing set up Pemberton-Billing Ltd – with "Supermarine" as its telegraphic address – Hubert became manager of the factory at Woolston, Hampshire.

In 1914 their first aircraft, the PB1, was exhibited at Olympia, where it was seen by Winston Churchill and King George V. Although orders were received from Germany, the war intervened and the plane never flew. In 1916 Pemberton Billing sold the company to Scott-Paine who registered it under the name Supermarine Aviation Company Limited. The company then concentrated on designing and building flying boats for the British Admiralty. Following the Armistice, Scott-Paine bought back 16 of his Supermarine Air Defence Flying Boats. He converted them for passenger service and, in February 1919, started the first cross-channel flying boat service, between Woolston and the Channel Islands and Le Havre. It was under his direction that Mitchell began building a series of seaplanes to compete for the Schneider Trophy.

After Scott-Paine sold Supermarine to Vickers-Armstrong, he helped set up Imperial Airways. He also ran the British Power Boat Company which built Miss England, the 27-foot racing boat, powered by a Napier Lion VIIA aero engine, that won back the Harmsworth Trophy from America in 1928; models are now on display in the Science Museum in London. During World War II, he made PT boats for the US Navy. After suffering a stroke, he became a US citizen at a special bedside sitting of the Superior Court. He died in 1954.

Above: Supermarine's owner Hugh Scott-Paine sold the company to build and race power boats, including the Harmsworth Trophy-winning Miss England.

Right: Hugh Scott-Paine did not give up his interest in flying. He is pictured here with his wife and the Duke of Sutherland at Lympne in Kent, home to air races in the 1930s.

With the takeover of Supermarine by Vickers-Armstrong in 1928, Supermarine remained essentially a separate entity – largely because Mitchell refused to let the parent company interfere with the work of his acclaimed design team that had already won the Schneider Trophy in 1922 with the Sea Lion II and in 1927 with the S6. The team continued its winning streak with the S6B and, even when all Vickers-Armstrong's other aviation interests were reorganized to become Vickers-Armstrong (Aircraft) Ltd in 1938, Supermarine continued to trade under its own name.

When Noel Pemberton Billing had founded the company in 1913 its aim was to build seaplanes – boats that flew rather than aircraft that floated. That was to change after the Sea Lion III was beaten by the Curtiss CR-3 floatplane at the 1923 Schneider Trophy race at Cowes. Mitchell's move into floatplanes would lead to the development of the Spitfire, Supermarine's first land plane.

Above: *The 450-horsepower Napier Lion engine that gave the Sea Lion a top speed of 160 miles per hour.*

Supermarine Sea Lion

The first Sea Lion was a development of the 1917 Supermarine Baby, a single-seat biplane with a wooden hull, modified specifically to take part in the 1919 Schneider Trophy race at Bournemouth. The race was abandoned due to fog and, later, the aircraft struck flotsam and sank.

R.J. Mitchell modified a 1920 Supermarine Sea King to make the Sea Lion II, which won the Schneider Trophy at Naples in 1922. The Sea King was a single-seat amphibian biplane powered by a 300-horsepower Hispano Suiza engine. Mitchell's Sea Lion used a 450-horsepower Napier Lion engine, which had a top speed of 160 miles per hour.

For the 1923 Schneider Race to be held at Cowes, Mitchell redesigned the aircraft with a 550-horsepower Napier Lion, producing Sea Lion III. But the aircraft only managed third place behind the Curtiss CR-3 and was transferred to the Royal Air Force in 1923.

Below: The Sea Lion III was redesigned with a 550-horsepower
Napier engine, but it could not match Glenn Curtiss's floatplanes.

Supermarine S5

After seeing the Curtiss CR-3, Mitchell abandoned the flying boat design in favour of the floatplane. His first effort was the Supermarine S4, a wooden racer powered by one 680-horsepower Napier Lion VII engine. On 13 September 1925 on Southampton Water it set a new world seaplane speed record at 226.752 miles per hour. However, it was wrecked during the trials in Baltimore before the 1925 Schneider Trophy in Chesapeake Bay.

Mitchell then designed a new all-metal monoplane racer with a low, braced wing, called the Supermarine S5. Three aircraft were built, one with a direct drive 900-horsepower Napier Lion VIIA engine, and the other two with a geared 875-horsepower Napier Lion VIIB engine. The S5s came first and second in the 1927 Schneider Trophy race held at Venice. The winning plane turned in an average speed of 281.66 miles per hour.

Another change had been made before 1927. The British followed the lead of the Italians and Americans and began using military pilots and the Air Ministry financed a British team drawn from the RAF, resulting in the formation of RAF High Speed Flight at the Marine Aircraft Experimental Establishment, Felixstowe.

Below: R.J. Mitchell was not slow to see that the floatplane could easily outperform the flying boat.

Supermarine S6

Mitchell decided that the Napier-engined S5 had reached the limit and redesigned the aircraft with a new 1,900-horsepower Rolls-Royce R engine as the Supermarine S6. Two aircraft were entered into the 1929 Schneider Trophy at Calshot. One was disqualified for turning inside one of the marker poles. The other won with an average speed of 328.63 miles per hour.

The government withdrew support for the next race due to be held in 1931 at Calshot on the Solent. The Royal Aero Club managed to raise several million pounds by public subscription. The benefactor Lady Houston and several newspapers put pressure on the British government who belatedly agreed to support the RAF's defence of the Trophy. Left with only nine months to prepare Supermarine's entry, Mitchell only had time to modify the S6 design to house a more powerful 2,350-horsepower version of the Rolls-Royce R engine. This became the Supermarine S6B, of which two were built. An upgraded S6, designated the S6A, was also entered. The winning flight turned in an average speed of 340.08 mph and the Schneider Trophy-winning S6B is now on display in the Science Museum in London. However, the achievement is slightly tarnished by the fact no other teams competed – the two S6Bs and the S6A were the only participants. Seventeen days later, the winning plane broke the world air-speed record reaching 407.5 miles per hour. The development of S6B is often said to have provided the impetus to develop both the Supermarine Spitfire and the Rolls-Royce Merlin engine.

Below: *Mitchell's floatplanes quickly put Supermarine back in contention in the Schneider Trophy.*

Chapter 4

On the Drawing Board

I n the years between World War I and World War II, there was a debate about the future of air power. The chief of the air staff, Air Marshal Hugh Trenchard was a committed bomber, who had organized a force of heavy bombers aimed to bomb Germany in the closing months of World War I. Earlier in the war, Trenchard had fallen out with Hugh Dowding, who would later head Fighter Command, and had him removed from front-line service by putting him in charge of training. However, Trenchard retired in 1929. The following year, Dowding joined the Air Council in charge of research and supply. Dowding was a vocal opponent of "Trenchardism", arguing that there was little point in bombing your enemy if you could not prevent him bombing you back.

Above: *Air Marshal Hugh Trenchard favoured bombers over fighters.*

What was needed, Dowding believed, was a fleet of high-speed, well-armed fighters. He thought that British aircraft manufacturers could capitalize on their success in the Schneider Trophy. However, once the Trophy was permanently in British hands, he opposed the Air Ministry proposals to host a new international competition on the grounds that "there was absolutely no value in floatplanes as a combat machine". Instead he wanted companies "to cash in on the experience that had been gained in aircraft construction and engine progress so that we could order two of the fastest machines which it was possible to build with no restrictions except landing speed, and that had to be on grass airfield". The two planes would become the Hurricane and the Spitfire.

Above: *Fortunately, the development of the Spitfire and the Hurricane was encouraged by Hugh Dowding, who went on to head Fighter Command.*

Air Marshal Hugh Dowding

Born in Dumfriesshire, Scotland, in 1882, Hugh Dowding joined the Royal Flying Corps in 1913, after he had obtained a pilot's licence. He rose to command a squadron in 1915 and was promoted to Air Vice Marshal in 1929. In September 1930, he joined the Air Council as air member for supply and research. One of his first acts was to sanction the certificate of airworthiness issued to the R101 airship, that crashed the next month. He was involved in the F7/30 Specification from its inception. He became an Air Marshal in 1933 and was knighted the following year.

In 1936, he was given command of the newly created Fighter Command. In this position, he vigorously promoted the development of the Spitfire, Hurricane and radar. During World War I, he had advocated the use of radio communication between pilots and ground controllers and claimed that he "was the first person in England, if not the world, to listen to a wireless telephone message from the air". As head of Fighter Command, he developed the "Dowding System" – an integrated air defence system of radar, raid plotting and radio control of aircraft. He was promoted to Air Chief Marshal in 1937.

Due to retire in June 1939, he stayed on. In 1940, he resisted repeated requests by Winston Churchill to send aircraft and pilots to aid Allied troops during the Battle of France, fearing that the resulting losses would weaken home defence. However, he helped organize air cover for the evacuation of the British Expeditionary Force at Dunkirk. During the Battle of Britain, Dowding's system successfully resisted the attacks of the Luftwaffe. He also maintained a significant fighter reserve, never committing more than half his force to the battle zone in southern England.

Although nicknamed "Stuffy" by his men, he was seen as a father figure who had the best interests of his men at heart. Indeed, his own son flew Spitfires with 74 Squadron. Credited with winning the Battle of Britain he was made a Knight Grand Cross of the Order of the Bath in October 1940. However, due to his temperament, he was removed from his post the following month and retired in November 1942. He was created a baron, but was passed over for promotion to the rank of marshal of the RAF, even when it was recognized that his victory in the Battle of Britain had been a turning point in the war.

The publication of his account, *Twelve Legions of Angels*, was suppressed in 1942. The book was finally published in 1946. In his retirement Dowding became actively interested in spiritualism and joined the Theosophical Society, a movement seeking the spiritual truth that underlay all religions. He published four books on the subject – *Many Mansions* (1943), *Lychgate* (1945), *God's Magic* (1946) and *The Dark Star* (1951). He became a vegetarian and espoused the cause of animal welfare. He also believed in fairies, flying saucers and communication with the dead, and insisted to his friend Lord Beaverbrook that he had been the leader of a Mongol tribe in a previous life. In *Lychgate* he wrote of meeting dead "RAF boys" in his sleep – these were spirits who flew fighters from mountain-top runways made of light. It was generally concluded that "Stuffy had gone a bit ga ga".

In later years, he became resentful of the way the RAF had treated him, though it was shown that some of his recollections were faulty. In 1968, he visited Hawkinge, an airfield near Folkestone, where the film *The Battle of Britain* (1969) was being shot. He met Laurence Olivier, who was playing him, on the set of his old office. Olivier told Dowding he had sat behind the desk all day "pretending to be you" and was "making an awful mess of it too". Dowding replied, "Oh, I'm sure you are". Olivier and the crew broke into laughter.

Dowding died at home on 15 February 1970. His ashes reside under the Battle of Britain memorial window in the RAF Chapel in Westminster Abbey. A statue of him was unveiled outside St Clement Danes, the RAF church in the Strand in London, in 1988.

Below: Air Marshal Hugh Dowding with legendary Battle of Britain pilot Douglas Bader and other officers under his command.

LYCHGATE
THE ENTRANCE TO THE PATH

AIR CHIEF MARSHAL
LORD DOWDING

These poor lads whose physical lives are suddenly blotted out in the heat of action, pass into the Astral, sometimes without even a moment of unconsciousness. They feel exactly as they did a moment before, they have (apparently) the same bodies and the same clothing; can you wonder if they fail to realize what has happened to them? They can generally still see and hear people who are yet in the flesh, though they cannot make themselves seen and heard.

On the other hand their vibrations are still on the Earth wavelength and they are consequently unable to see or hear the Helpers or Messengers or their relations or comrades who have come to meet them.

Left: Dowding was plainly disturbed by the number of young men he had sent to their deaths. In later life, he wrote a number of books about spiritualism, leading some to suppose he had lost his wits.

In 1930, under Dowding's aegis, the Air Ministry issued Specification F7/30 calling for a new fighter, capable of 250 miles per hour, armed with four machine guns. Supermarine were now well connected with the Air Ministry through the sale of the Southampton and the use of the RAF High Speed Flight to pilot the entrants to the Schneider Trophy. By then, fulfilling Specification F7/30 was well within Supermarine's capability as the S6 had already topped 328 miles per hour.

The selection was made at a competition held in February 1934. The competitors were the Blackburn F3, Bristol Type 123, Bristol Type 133, Gloster Gladiator, Gloster SS19, Hawker PV3, Westland F7/30 and Supermarine Type 224. This was a single-seat all-metal monoplane built using a modern metal stressed skin construction. Powered by a 660-horsepower steam-cooled Rolls-Royce Goshawk engine, it had an inverted gull wing with a span of 45 feet 10 inches.

Below: The Supermarine Type 224 failed in the competition to win a fighter contract from the Air Ministry, but it had many of the makings of the Spitfire.

Rolls-Royce Goshawk Engine

Developed by Rolls-Royce as the Kestrel IV, it featured evaporative cooling and was renamed the Goshawk. A small number of these inline piston engines were built and were used only in prototypes and various one-offs. Powers for individual installations are quoted between 650 and 700 horsepower. It was the power unit specified for the twin-engined Short Knuckleduster, built to Specification R24/31 of a "general purpose open-sea patrol flying boat", but lost out to the Supermarine Stranraer, and was the "preferred" engine for the Blackburn F3 biplane night-fighter, Bristol Type 123 interceptor, Hawker PV3 biplane, Westland PV4 biplane and Supermarine Type 224, all built to Specification F7/30. It also powered the private venture Hawker "Intermediate Fury" single-seat prototype and the Westland Pterodactyl V, an experimental two-seat turret fighter carrying two Vickers machine guns built to Specification F5/33, which was later cancelled. It was installed for trials in the Gloster TSR38, the first prototype Gloster Gnatsnapper naval deck-landing biplane fighter built to Specification N21/26 and the Hawker High Speed Fury, built to test design features for the PV3. The Goshawk was found to be unreliable and a Kestrel engine was substituted.

Above: The Rolls-Royce Goshawk engine – many of its shortcomings were reflected in the design of the Supermarine Type 224.

Steam from the Goshawk engine was condensed in the wing's leading edge and the water collected in tanks in the strange "trousers" of its fixed undercarriage. The innovative design of the Type 224 was not reflected in its performance. It had a maximum speed of only 228 miles per hour and took 9.5 minutes to climb to 15,000 feet. The winner was a biplane – the prototype Gloster Gladiator. It had a top speed of 242 miles per hour and could reach 15,000 feet in 6.5 minutes.

The steam condensation system was unreliable. The cockpit was open and the Type 224 had no flaps. This meant that it would have had to land at high speed, making it difficult to land safely at night. The Air Ministry's specification had called for an aircraft that could function as a fighter both day and night.

Dowding was particularly disappointed in Mitchell's design and irritated by the Type 224 drag-inducing trousered undercarriage. "There is no reason why Supermarine should not have included retractable undercarriage and flaps in their original design," he wrote to Air Commodore Cave-Brown-Cave in August 1934.

By this time Hitler was in power in Germany and aiming to step up German airpower, leaving Dowding exasperated at the British manufacturers' failure to come up with a satisfactory prototype. He wrote in an Air Ministry report in 1934: "The time has come when we must apply the screws."

Earlier that year it had even been suggested that the Air Ministry should buy the PZL's P24 fighter from Poland to fulfil F7/30. "The P24 is four miles per hour faster than the Supermarine and climbs 15,000 feet in two and a half minutes less," read a study.

Right: *Poland's PZL P24 was rejected by the Air Ministry purely for strategic reasons. Had it been chosen, the outcome of World War II could have been very different.*

The PZL P24

The PZL P24 was developed as an export version of the PZL P11, a gull-wing all-metal fighter designed by Zygmunt Pulawski and built in the company's factory in Warsaw. The P11 had been powered with a Bristol Mercury engine built under licence. But the licence did not permit export sales, so the first P24 prototype was powered by a French Gnome-Rhône 14Kds 760-horsepower Mistral Major engine. Unfortunately the engine shook the propeller off, though the pilot landed the plane safely. The second P24 prototype, named the "Super P24", set a world speed record for radial engine-powered fighters of 257.24 miles per hour. The third P24 prototype was the "Super P24bis" and had a more powerful 14Kfs engine and a three-blade propeller. It attracted a great deal of attention at the 1934 Paris air show, though it could not be entered into the competition for a new French fighter due to objections from the French aircraft industry.

In the meantime, a new version of the P11, the P11c, was developed for the Polish Air Force. It had a newly streamlined fuselage, with the radial engine lowered to give the pilot a better view. These changes were adopted by the new P24 prototype, flown in 1936, which used the whole tail fuselage section from the P11c. It was powered by a Gnome-Rhône 14Kfs 930-horsepower engine and was armed with two 20-mm Oerlikon FF cannon and two 7.92-mm Colt-Browning machine guns. This entered production as the P24A. The P24B version was armed with four machine guns and the P24C was armed with four machine guns and two 50-kilogram bombs. The P24A and P24B could also carry four 12.5-kilogram bombs. Other versions were planned, but could not be delivered due to the war.

The aircraft had an all-metal construction with high gull wings. In the production models, it had a closed canopy. It had conventional fixed landing gear, with a rear skid. The fuel tank could be dropped in case of fire. It was 35 feet 1 inch long and had a wingspan of 24 feet 7 inches. Its top speed was 270 miles per hour and it had a range of 340 miles. Its ceiling in service was 34,449 feet and it had a rate of climb of 2,260 feet a minute.

Although the P24 was a better fighter than the P11, the Polish Air Force did not take it, preferring to wait for the PZL P50. When it became clear that this would not be ready in time to counter the German attack, the PAF resumed the order for the P24, but none were ready to fight in the Polish Campaign in 1939. The aircraft had greater success abroad, though. The PZL P24 was the main Greek fighter at the time of the Italian attack in 1940, and shot down 40 Italian planes. One P24 was captured by Italians and was taken for testing in Centro Sperimentale de Volo near Rome. However, it proved no match for the Luftwaffe when the Germans invaded in 1941. Four German planes were shot down but, in all, 35 Greek P24s were lost. The last remaining Greek P24 flew from Crete to Egypt with six Westland Lysanders of the RAF's 208 Squadron on 23 April 1941.

The Romanians built some under licence and used some components, notably the tail section, in their own IAR 80, a low-winged fighter. The Turks used P24s for training until the late 1940s. Some were refitted with Pratt & Whitney Twin Wasp engines. The only surviving example of a PZL P24 in the world is a museum piece in Turkey, seen variously in museums in Ankara and Istanbul.

In the end, the Air Ministry rejected the P24. For strategic reasons they had to buy British and there were doubts that even the P24 was sufficiently advanced. Instead they ordered the Gloster Gladiator. It was one of the few entrants that did not use the Rolls-Royce Goshawk engine. Instead it used the 850-horsepower Bristol Mercury IX radial engine. It is thought that the Bristol Type 133, also powered by Bristol Mercury, would have won if the prototype had not been lost in an accident.

Even before the Type 224 was rejected, Mitchell had begun work on the Type 300. This would become the Spitfire.

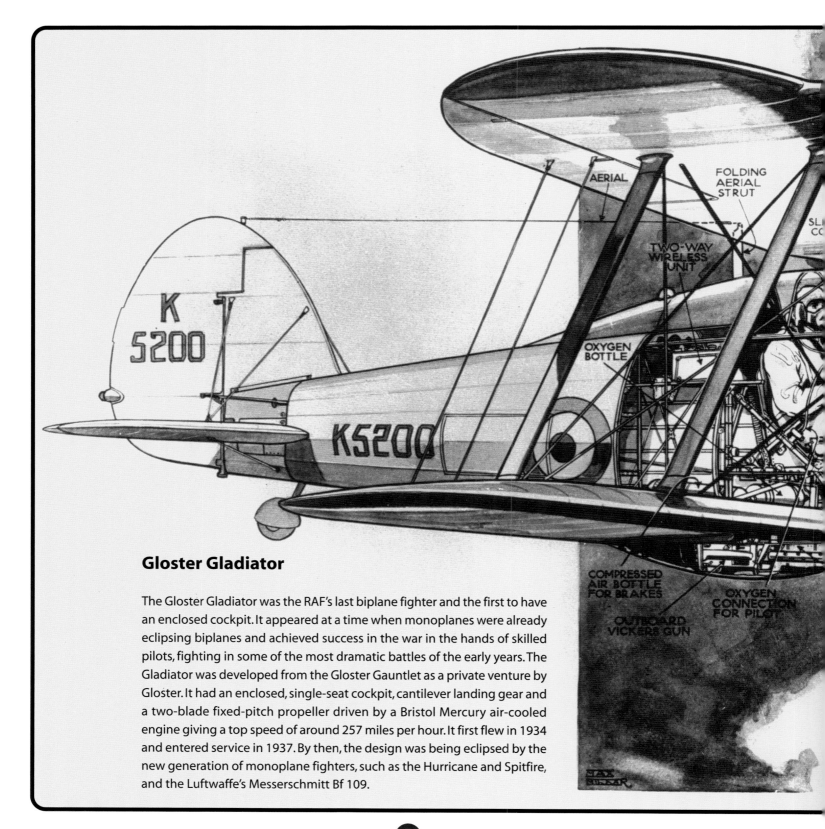

Gloster Gladiator

The Gloster Gladiator was the RAF's last biplane fighter and the first to have an enclosed cockpit. It appeared at a time when monoplanes were already eclipsing biplanes and achieved success in the war in the hands of skilled pilots, fighting in some of the most dramatic battles of the early years. The Gladiator was developed from the Gloster Gauntlet as a private venture by Gloster. It had an enclosed, single-seat cockpit, cantilever landing gear and a two-blade fixed-pitch propeller driven by a Bristol Mercury air-cooled engine giving a top speed of around 257 miles per hour. It first flew in 1934 and entered service in 1937. By then, the design was being eclipsed by the new generation of monoplane fighters, such as the Hurricane and Spitfire, and the Luftwaffe's Messerschmitt Bf 109.

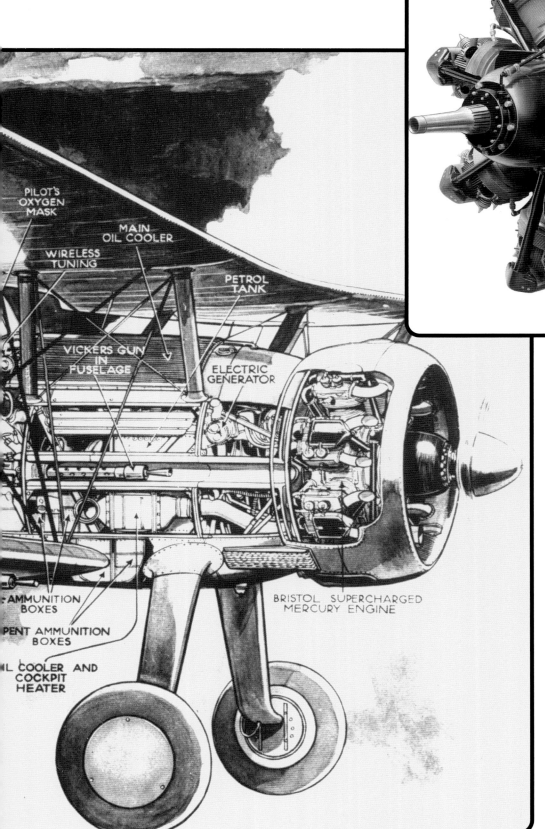

Above: *The Bristol Mercury III radial engine.*

PILOT'S
OXYGEN
MASK

MAIN
OIL COOLER

WIRELESS
TUNING

PETROL
TANK

VICKERS GUN
IN
FUSELAGE

ELECTRIC
GENERATOR

AMMUNITION
BOXES

PENT AMMUNITION
BOXES

IL COOLER AND
COCKPIT
HEATER

BRISTOL SUPERCHARGED
MERCURY ENGINE

Left: *The Gloster Gladiator, picked over the Supermarine Type 224 and the PZL P24.*

Gladiators were also modified for carrier operations and flown by the Royal Navy's Fleet Air Arm as the Sea Gladiator. A total of 747 airframes were built – some 483 for the RAF and 98 for the RN – while 216 were exported, some from the RAF's allotment, to some 13 countries, including Belgium, China, Egypt, Finland, Free France, Greece, Iraq, Ireland, Latvia, Lithuania, Norway, Portugal, South Africa and Sweden.

They saw action in almost all theatres during World War II, with a large number of air forces, some of them on the Axis side. The RAF used them in France, Norway, Greece, the defence of Malta and during the invasion of Iraq in 1941, where they saw action against other Gladiators flown by the Royal Iraqi Air Force. China used Gladiators to fight the Japanese from 1938. The Finns and Swedish volunteers flew them against the Soviet Union from 1939 to 1944, and Norway, Belgium and Greece used them to resist the Axis invasion.

Left: *Gloster Gladiators going into action. Despite their dated biplane design, they continued in use throughout World War II.*

The Gladiator was 27 feet 5 inches long with a wingspan of 32 feet 3 inches. They were not made of stressed steel like Spitfires or Hurricanes. Instead, they had taut canvas wings, covered with inflammable dope, stretched over a wooden frame, making them extremely vulnerable to fire. The range was 444 miles, with a ceiling of 33,500 feet and a rate of climb of 2,220 feet per minute compared with the Type 224's 1,578 feet per minute.

It was armed with four synchronized .303-inch Browning machine guns, one on each side of the fuselage and one beneath each lower wing. In some Sea Gladiators, a pair of Brownings were fitted under the upper wings as well, bringing the total to six. The upper wing Brownings were often fitted in the field, in particular during the defence of Malta.

Above: *The cockpit of the Gloster Gladiator could be a death trap as the wood and canvas construction was vulnerable to fire.*

Bristol Type 133

A private venture designed for the F7/30 competition, the Type 133 single-seat monoplane featured a forward fuselage of girder-type construction, a monocoque rear fuselage and stressed skinning. It was 28 feet long with a wingspan of 39 feet and a top speed of 260 miles per hour. It was powered by a Bristol Mercury VIS.2 rated at 620 horsepower for take-off and carrying an armament of two synchronized .303-inch Vickers guns in the fuselage and a Lewis gun of similar calibre mounted above each main wheel housing. The Type 133 flew for the first time on 8 June 1934. After completing a considerable amount of flying, on 8 March 1935 the prototype went into a flat spin. The engine stopped, the pilot bailed out, and the aircraft was destroyed. No further development was undertaken.

Left: The Gloster Gladiator had Browning machine guns mounted under the lower wings as standard. Sea Gladiators had them fitted under the upper wings as well.

Chapter 5

The Spitfire Emerges

Mitchell himself was dissatisfied with the Type 224 and set about a radical redesign. To reach the heights and speeds required the plane would have to be less bulky. He began by chopping almost six feet off the wingspan. Flaps were added, along with a new tailplane and elevator. The oil and cooler tanks were placed under the engines. The cockpit was enclosed and a retractable undercarriage was fitted. These modifications promised to give the new plane, the Type 300, a top speed of 265 miles per hour.

Right: *This recently constructed replica shows the smooth lines of the monocoque design.*

Below: *K5054 was the prototype Spitfire that first took to the air on 5 March 1936.*

Left: Later, the Mark IX Spitfire was fitted with a four-blade propeller.

Above: The carburettor air intake was fitted under the central fuselage.

Right: Visibility through the Spitfire's clear blown canopy had advantages over the Bf 109's heavily framed cockpit canopy.

Left: The radiator was located beneath the starboard wing while the smaller oil cooler was beneath the port wing, causing some asymmetry.

The new plane would have to be made as a private venture. After all, the Air Ministry had already spent £18,000 on the development of the Type 224. The Ministry's reluctance to extend Supermarine's budget to take in the modification is sometimes seen as an indication that they were not impressed with the redesign. But they were. The problem was that the changes were so far-reaching that they could not be accepted under the current F7/30 Specification. Such a move would be unfair to the other companies bidding. So the director of technical development, Air Commodore Henry Cave-Brown-Cave suggested ordering it as an experimental aircraft outside F7/30. In August 1934, he wrote to Dowding, saying: "I think it would be a wise precaution to order one of these modified F7/30s from Supermarine if they will quote a reasonable price and delivery. It will be a suitable type on which to overcome many of the problems we shall have later… It will also be a most interesting experiment with wing flaps on a high performance plane."

Left: *The wing bolt of the original Spitfire prototype that has been made into a hammer head, now in the Solent Sky museum in Southampton.*

Dowding agreed and on 4 September 1934, the Contracts Section of the Air Ministry wrote asking Supermarine to submit a quotation for the new modified fighter:

"The Department requests that you will inform them as soon as possible what will be the cost and time for the delivery of the new aeroplane," they wrote. "I am to add that the request for a quotation must not be taken as indicative of any intention on the part of the Department to order such a plane."

Air Commodore Henry Cave-Brown-Cave

Born on 1 February 1887, he joined the Navy as an Engineering Officer, transferred to the Royal Navy Air Service and got his pilot's licence on 20 March 1915. He was partly responsible for devising the idea of attaching the fuselage of a BE2c to the underside of a Willows airship, creating RNAS's first successful non-rigid airship. In 1927 he was selected to form and lead the RAF's Far East Flight. The Flight flew a total of 27,950 miles to Singapore. His active career came to a premature end when he was injured in an air crash on 17 January 1939, in which his PA was killed. Air Vice-Marshal Cave-Brown-Cave CB DSO AFC died on 5 August 1965.

Below: Mitchell's prototype K5054, first rolled out on public display at the Hendon Air Pageant, 27 June 1936.

Below: The Spitfire's first bill.

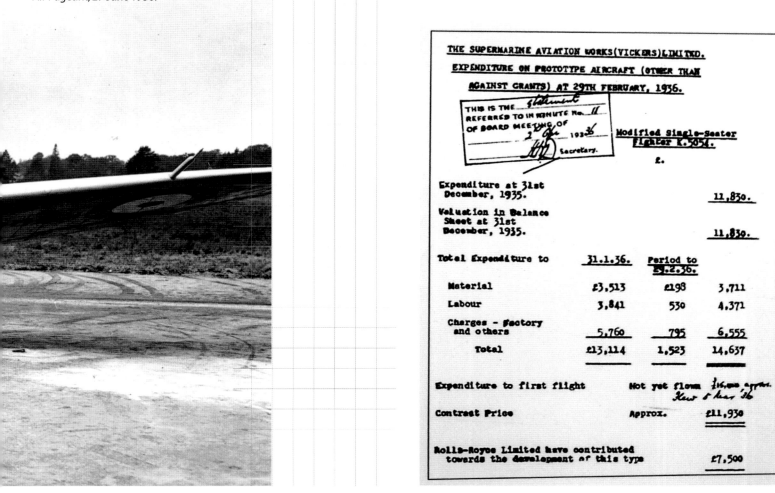

Vickers were particularly generous towards Supermarine's new project as Vickers Aircraft itself had invested time and money on its own single-engine fighters, the "Jockey", and then the "Venom", which were still in the running for an Air Ministry production order.

Vickers Jockey

During the mid 1920s, the Air Ministry believed that the primary role of fighters was the interception of enemy bombers. They drew up Specification F20/27 for a single-seat day interceptor capable of overtaking an enemy aircraft flying at 150 miles per hour at 20,000 feet. Monoplanes from de Havilland, Westland and Vickers contended. The Vickers Type 151 was built on the principles of all-metal construction developed in France by Wibaul, though the rear of the fuselage was covered with fabric. It was powered by a nine-cylinder Bristol Mercury IIA radial engine rated at 480 horsepower at 13,000 feet and carried twin .303-inch Vickers guns. The Type 151 first flew in April 1930, but there were problems with the rigidity of the rear fuselage. In January 1932 the rear fuselage was redesigned and a 530-horsepower Jupiter VIIF engine added. There were plans to redesign the plane around a Mercury IVS2 supercharged engine, but in June 1932 the prototype crashed while undergoing trials at Martlesham Heath. The plane was then redesigned as the Jockey II, then adapted to meet Specification F5/34 for a high-performance fighter with an air-cooled engine for use in hot climates as the Vickers Venom.

Below: *With the war clouds gathering over Europe, the race was on to build a fighter that could protect the skies over Britain.*

Vickers Venom

After the Type 151 Vickers Jockey was redesigned and improved as the Type 279 Jockey II, it was submitted under Air Ministry Specification F.5/34 as the Vickers Venom, beginning its test flights on 17 June 1936. It had a metal monocoque fuselage whose stressed skin was joined with countersunk rivets and 90-degree deflection flaps – a unique feature at the time. The Venom retained the sideways-hinging engine feature of the Type 151, and a battery of eight .303-inch machine guns was mounted in the wings. The plane proved exceptionally manoeuvrable, with an outstanding roll rate and turning radius. However, its 625-horsepower Bristol Aquila AE.3S nine-cylinder sleeve-valve radial engine lacked the power to compete with Rolls-Royce liquid-cooled V-engine contemporaries. As no compact air-cooled radial with power could be found, the Venom was scrapped in 1939.

Below: Vickers aircraft division competed with its subsidiary Supermarine for the Air Ministry's fighter contracts.

Mitchell pressed on with his design, further shortening the wingspan, slimming the wings and adopting stressed-skin construction. But these alterations would yield only slight improvements in performance. The central problem remained the 660-horsepower Goshawk engine, which meant that the design had to include a strong metal leading edge in front of the wing spar to act as the condensation tank for the steam cooling. He considered substituting the new Napier Dagger engine. But, at just 700 horsepower, the change hardly seemed worthwhile.

The Napier Dagger Engine

The Napier Dagger was a 24-cylinder H-pattern air-cooled engine designed by Frank Halford, based on the earlier Napier Rapier. Its H design allowed it to have more small cylinders which should give more power and higher revs for the same frontal profile as a large liquid-cooled V engine. It was essentially two vertically opposed inline engines lying side by side. The opposed cylinders gave very smooth running and the Dagger was remarkable for its fast rotation, running at up to 4,000 revs per minute. Although it was considered a masterpiece of design, there were problems with cooling, maintenance, weight and manufacture, which were never satisfactorily overcome. The Dagger powered the Hawker Hector biplane and the Handley Page Hereford bomber. Because of the problem of engine cooling, the Hector could not be used in the tropics, and the Hereford was unsuitable for combat because its Dagger VIII engines were noisy and unreliable. The Dagger was also used in the experimental Martin-Baker MB 2 fighter, development of which ended in 1938.

Then Rolls-Royce began working on a new aero engine, known initially as the PV12. It had been in development since 1932 and already gave 800 horsepower at 12,000 feet and, with further development, looked like it could exceed 1,000 hp. It was the brain-child of Ernest Hives, whose R series engines had powered Supermarine's Schneider Trophy winners. Consequently, Supermarine had an excellent relationship with Rolls-Royce and reached an agreement for the new engine to power Mitchell's redesigned fighter.

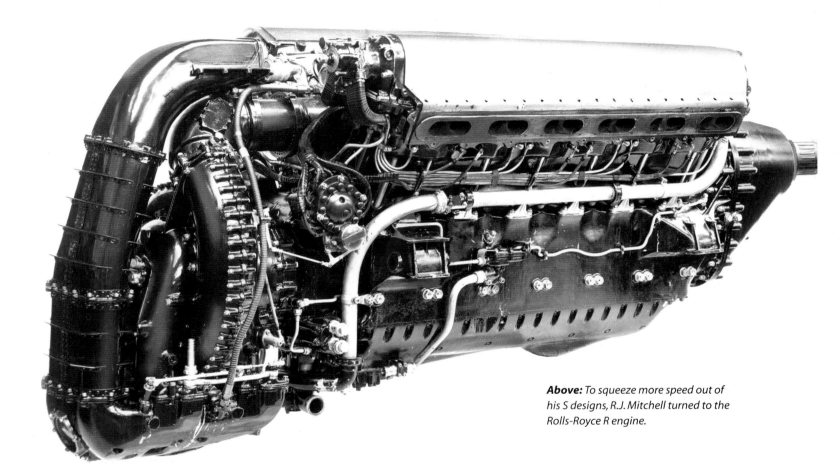

Above: To squeeze more speed out of his S designs, R.J. Mitchell turned to the Rolls-Royce R engine.

Left: While aircraft manufacturers competed with fighter designs, engine makers fought to come up with a powerplant that was both powerful and reliable.

Ernest Hives

Born in Reading in 1886, Hives was the twelfth child of a factory clerk and started work in a local garage in 1898. In 1903, after fixing Charles Stewart Rolls' car he got a job in the garage of Rolls' car dealership. In 1908 Hives became one of the company's chief test drivers, leading the Rolls-Royce team in the Austrian Alpine Trial in 1913. At the beginning of World War I, Hives helped develop the company's first aero engine, the Eagle, and by 1916 he was Head of the Experimental Department, working on the Kestrel and the R series, used in Supermarine's Schneider Trophy winners in 1929 and 1931. When Henry Royce died in 1933, Hives completed the development of the Merlin engine.

In 1936 he became the general works manager of the Rolls-Royce factory. The following year he joined the board. In 1937, believing that war was inevitable, he prepared the firm for a massive increase in the production of Merlin engines. As Merlins powered both Hurricanes and Spitfires, this was a decision of vital strategic significance. In 1941, Hives decided to commit the company to the development of the gas turbine, ensuring the company's leading role in the production of jet engines. He became managing director in 1946 and chairman of Rolls-Royce from 1950 to 1956. He died in 1965.

When the new Rolls-Royce PV12 engine – later to be renamed the Merlin – was substituted for the Goshawk, the strong metal leading edge was retained because the Merlin was originally envisaged as having steam cooling like the Goshawk, though it would also have a small back-up radiator. The first few Mark A and B Merlins used this composite cooling system, but the Mark C and all subsequent Merlins switched to an all-liquid system using ethylene glycol. This transferred heat better than water and hence meant the radiators could be made smaller. Although the strong leading edge of the Spitfire's wing was no longer needed as a condenser tank, it was retained. It had come about by chance, but the metal leading edge "box" in front of the main spar of the wing added to its strength and was the key to the success of the final aircraft.

To make the wings thin, the inverted gull-wing shape had been ditched. Mitchell then changed to the distinctive elliptical shape, which made the plane instantly recognizable.

Below left: The Rolls-Royce Eagle engine, the company's first foray into aero engines.

Below: R.J. Mitchell and Henry Royce collaborated for over ten years, developing the various forerunners to the Spitfire.

Rolls-Royce

In 1884, Frederick Henry Royce started an electrical and mechanical business. He made his first car – a "Royce" – in his Manchester factory in 1904. That year he met car dealer Charles Stewart Rolls who signed an exclusive deal to sell Royce's cars. The contract said the cars would be called "Rolls-Royce". The company was formed in 1906, and began manufacturing the Silver Ghost. It moved to Derby in 1908, and in 1921 a second factory in Springfield, Massachusetts, helped meet demand. The chassis of the Silver Ghost was used for the first British armoured car used in both world wars.

The company moved into aero engines in 1914 with the Eagle. Around half the aircraft engines supplied to the Allies in World War I were made by Rolls-Royce. In 1919 the Eagle powered a twin-engined Vickers Vimy bomber on the first direct flight across the Atlantic. By the late 1920s, aero engines made up most of the company's business. Before Henry Royce died in 1933, he began work on the Merlin engine, which he developed after his R engine had powered a record-breaking Supermarine S6B seaplane to over 400 miles per hour in 1931. The Merlin was a powerful V12 engine. It went into production in 1935 and was fitted into many World War II aircraft, including the single-engined Hawker Hurricane and the Spitfire, the twin-engined de Havilland Mosquito and Vickers Wellington, and four-engined Avro Lancaster. Built in the US by Packard under licence, it made the P-51 Mustang into one of the best fighters of its time. Developed as the Meteor, it was also used to power the Centurion tank and other military vehicles. Over 160,000 Merlin engines were produced.

Right: *The Lancaster Bomber was also powered by the Rolls-Royce Merlin engine.*

This brought several advantages. Beverly Shenstone, the Canadian-born aerodynamicist who worked with Mitchell throughout the development of the Spitfire, said:"Aerodynamically it was the best for our purpose because the induced drag, caused in producing lift, was lowest when this shape was used: the ellipse was an ideal shape, theoretically perfection."

Beverly Shenstone

Born in Canada in 1906, Beverly Strachan Shenstone spent his entire career in aircraft research and development. In 1929, he joined with Junkers in Germany. Then, in 1932, he moved to Supermarine where he worked on the Spitfire from its inception. His flare for aerodynamics helped perfect the plane's iconic elliptical wing. During World War II, he worked in aircraft design and production for the Air Commission. Afterwards, he was a consultant to several large aircraft companies, including A.V. Roe (Canada), British European Airways, British Overseas Airways Corporation and Canadair, where he contributed to the design of the Northstar aircraft. He was President of the Royal Aeronautical Society for 1962–63 and died in 1978.

It also meant that it had a wing chord – that is, the distance between the leading edge of the wing and the trailing edge – that tapered only slightly towards the tip. Consequently, there was plenty of room inside the wing for the retractable undercarriage and the aircraft's guns. The wheels retracted outwards into the wing, so the lifting mechanism could be put in the thickest part of the wing, keeping the rest of the wing thin. The undercarriage retracted into bays to the rear of the wing spar, meaning the structural integrity of the leading edge "box" was not impaired.

The design work was well advanced when the RAF asked for an armament of eight machine guns in all new fighter aircraft. Over at the Hawker aircraft company, Sydney Camm, who was designing the Hurricane, had no problems fitting the guns close together in the thick wing of his fighter. But Mitchell also managed with the Spitfire's thin wings. As he had adopted the elliptical shape, he could spread out the machine guns and their ammunition boxes along the wing, accommodating four machine guns in each wing rather than the two originally envisioned.

The new wing was given a slight twist, so that the angle to the air flow was slightly greater near the fuselage than at the tip. It meant that any stall would begin near the root of the wing. As a result, the pilot got plenty of warning of a stall, via feedback to the controls. This was particularly important in combat as, in a tight turn, the aircraft needs to be kept just on the edge of stalling to get the minimum turning circle.

Left: *The de Havilland Mosquito benefited from the reliability of the Merlin too.*

Jeffrey Quill

Born in 1913, Jeffrey Quill was inspired to fly when he saw several aeroplanes land near his home in Sussex when he was five. At 18, he joined the RAF, going solo after just five hours and twenty minutes' training. Judged an exceptional flier, he heard that "Mutt" Summers at Vickers wanted an assistant to test fly new planes, including the Type 300 – Spitfire. Released from the RAF, he joined Vickers on 6 January 1936 and on 6 March flew Summers to Eastleigh to test fly the Spitfire. Quill then transferred to Supermarine, where he completed the Spitfire's test flights.

Below: Test pilot Jeffrey Quill in the cockpit of a Spitfire with fellow test pilot Dave Morgan standing on the wing and Gordon Monger of design staff.

With the fall of France, he returned to the RAF, flying Spitfires with 65 Squadron during the Battle of Britain and shooting down two enemy planes. Returning to Supermarine, he became chief test pilot. In 1943, he served with the Fleet Air Arm, helping to develop better carrier-deck landing with the Seafire, the naval version of the Spitfire. Quill made the first flights and masterminded the development and production test flying of all 52 variants of the Spitfire. He also made the first flights of the Dumbo, an experimental variable-incidence wing torpedo bomber; the Spiteful; the Seafang; and, in July 1946, the Attacker, the Royal Navy's first jet fighter.

After 5,000 hours of flying in 90 different types of aircraft, Quill retired as a test pilot to become sales manager of Supermarine, then Vickers-Armstrong (Aircraft), then the British Aircraft Corporation. He took similar positions with the Anglo-French company developing the Jaguar supersonic combat aircraft and the Anglo-German-Italian consortium developing the Tornado swing-wing fighter. He retired in 1978 and died in 1996.

Far Left: *Gifts given to Jeffrey Quill by Supermarine to commemorate his first flights.*

Above: *The Seafang, a marine version of the Spitfire, also test flown by Jeffrey Quill.*

"The Spitfire's extremely docile behaviour in the stall was one of its greatest features," said assistant test pilot Jeffrey Quill. "You could pull it well beyond its buffer boundary and drag it around with full power and little airspeed; it would shudder and shake and rock you from side to side, but if you handled it properly it would never get away from you. Whether they knew it or not, there are many pilots alive today who owe their survival to this remarkable quality in the Spitfire – and I am one of them."

Above: *The prototype K5054 takes to the air.*

The Spitfire's wing turned out to be capable of withstanding very high Mach numbers. In fact, the wing's performance at high speed was better than the wings designed for the early jet fighters ten years later.

Mitchell gave the Type 300 a monocoque fuselage, which meant that the interior was not obstructed by bracing struts or wires. This was in contrast to the Hurricane, which had a fuselage constructed like a fabric-covered biplane. The space inside the Spitfire allowed large cameras to be mounted behind the pilot, pointing downwards and to the side for photo-reconnaissance missions.

The Spitfire's fuel tank was mounted between the engine and the pilot. The Spitfire was not originally designed to carry fuel in the wings. Fuel was only put in the wings – in small tanks in the leading edge – for reconnaissance Spitfires where no guns were carried or in models made late in the war. Photo-reconnaissance models needed a longer range; standard Spitfires were restricted to a short range. At that time all single-seat fighters, with the exception of the Japanese Zero, had the same problem. The Allies had to wait for the later Mustang and Thunderbolt before they had fighters that had a range of 1,000 miles or more.

Below: *From the first flights of the prototype it was clear that the Spitfire was a remarkable aeroplane.*

Zero

The A6M Zero was the premier Japanese fighter aircraft during World War II. Its development began in May 1937, soon after the introduction of the Mitsubishi A5M fighter. It was a joint venture by Mitsubishi and Nakajima to produce a new carrier-based fighter under the Imperial Japanese Navy's Specification "12-Shi". The updated specifications called for a fighter carrying two 20-mm cannon as well as two .303-inch machine guns. It should be capable of 310 miles per hour at 13,000 feet, with an endurance of two hours at normal power and six to eight hours at cruising speed with drop tanks. Each airplane was also to have a radio set and a radio direction finder for navigation. As the plane was to be carrier-based, its wingspan was restricted to 39 feet.

When the Japanese Navy's final specification was published, Nakajima pulled out, believing that it was impossible to build such an aircraft. But after some initial testing, Mitsubishi's chief designer, Jiro Horikoshi, determined that the Navy's requirements could be met. To meet the specification the aircraft would have to be extremely light. Using a new, top-secret aluminium alloy, T-7178, he designed an aircraft of unprecedented lightness and speed. To do so, he had to sacrifice armour to protect the pilot and the self-sealing fuel tanks that were becoming standard on military aircraft. A low-wing monoplane with retractable landing gear, the A6M was one of the world's most manoeuvrable fighters when it completed testing.

Above: *The Japanese Zero was a first class fighter but, unlike the Spitfire and American planes, its design did not develop during the war and it found itself outgunned and outclassed.*

It entered service in 1940 as the Type 0 Carrier Fighter – hence, the "Zero". Eleven Zeros arrived in China where they quickly proved themselves in conflict. Fitted with a new 950-horsepower Nakajima Sakae 12 engine, the aircraft exceeded its design specifications and a new version with folding wing-tips, the A6M2, Model 21, went into production for use on carriers. During World War II, the Model 21 was the version of the Zero that was most often encountered by Allied aviators. Early in the war, the Zero was able to out-manoeuvre its opposition as it was a superior dogfighter than early Allied fighters. But Allied pilots quickly developed new tactics for dealing with the Zero. These included the "boom-and-zoom", where Allied pilots attacked on the dive or climb, and the "Thach weave", devised by John S. Thach of the US Navy, where two Allied pilots worked in tandem. These tactics worked because of the Zero's complete lack of protection – a single burst of fire was generally enough to down the aircraft. In contrast, American fighters, such as the F4F Wildcat and the P40 Warhawk, though less manoeuvrable, were extremely rugged and difficult to bring down. Nevertheless, Zeros downed at least 1,550 American planes between 1941 and 1945. However, the Zero was never substantially updated or replaced. With the introduction of new Allied fighters, such as the F6F Hellcat and F4U Corsair, the Zero was quickly outclassed and its kill ratio dropped from 1:1 to over 1:10. During the course of the war, over 11,000 A6M Zeros were produced.

While the Type 300 was developed primarily as a high-speed technology demonstrator to push forward aircraft design, the Air Ministry soon realized that the new aircraft would be suitable for production as a front-line fighter. They drew up Specification F10/35 around the Type 300, considerably reducing their normal requirements for fuel capacity and range. The Air Ministry was so enthusiastic about Mitchell's design that they even put up the money to build the prototype.

Mitchell devoted most of 1935 to work on the Type 300, along with Beverly Shenstone who worked on the wing design and Alfred Faddy who did much of the detailed design work. The directors of Supermarine were thinking of calling their new fighter the Shrew. The name Spitfire was suggested by Sir Robert MacLean, director of Vickers-Armstrong at the time, who called his daughter Ann "a little spitfire". The word, originating in the 17th century, originally meant that which "spits fire" – a cannon or a hot-tempered creature. Mitchell's sister-in-law Elsie remembered him saying, "Just the sort of bloody silly name they would choose".

The Spitfire prototype, with the serial number K5054, first flew from Eastleigh Aerodrome – now Southampton airport – on 5 March 1936. It was piloted by Vicker's chief test pilot "Mutt" Summers who reported that it handled beautifully. His assistant Jeffrey Quill took over on 26 March. In later tests, it reached 349 miles per hour. This time Mitchell, who had already retired, had delivered the goods. Even before the prototype had completed its official trials the RAF ordered 310 and the success of Mitchell's fighter was assured.

Above: The K5054 prototype provoked intense interest when displayed at air shows.

Left: The prototype Spitfire gets a royal visit.

Captain Joe "Mutt" Summers

Born around 1903 – his birth certificate was never found – Joseph Summers joined the RAF in 1924, flying Sopwith Snipes and Gloster Grebes. After only six months he was posted as a test pilot to the Aircraft and Armament Experimental Establishment at Martlesham Heath, Suffolk, where he acquired the nickname "Mutt". At Martlesham, he repeatedly risked his life testing new planes, including the Gloster Gamecock, Bristol Bulldog, Hawker Hornbill and Avro Avenger. In 1929, he was appointed chief test pilot to Vickers (Aviation) Ltd and, when Vickers took over Supermarine, he became chief test pilot for both companies. On 6 March 1936, he flew K5054 – the prototype Supermarine Spitfire – for the first time. After a 15-minute flight, Summers landed and declared: "I don't want anything touched."

During World War II, Summers helped Vickers' chief designer Neville Barnes Wallis develop the bouncing bomb used by the Dambusters. After the war he tested the Vickers Viscount, the first turbo-prop passenger plane, and the Vickers Valiant, the first V bomber. He retired in 1951 and died in 1954.

Right: "Mutt" Summers of Vickers with 1931 Schneider Trophy-winner John Boothman, now Air Vice Marshal.

The era of the monoplane piston-engined fighter lasted only some 15 years, from about 1935 to 1950. The Spitfire was unique in that it was the only aircraft to span this whole period and was the only plane to fly before, during and after World War II.

Development of the Hurricane

In 1933, Hawker's chief designer, Sydney Camm, began designing an aircraft to fulfil Air Ministry Specification F36/34 for a new monoplane fighter. His prototype, powered by a 990-horsepower Rolls-Royce Merlin C engine, first flew on 6 November 1935, and quickly surpassed expectations. The first aircraft had fabric-covered wings. Official trials began in February 1936 and in June Hawker got an initial order for 600 aircraft from the RAF. The production model was to be powered by the new 1,030-horsepower Merlin II engine.

The first production Hurricane flew on 12 October 1937, and the first batch was delivered to the 111 Squadron at RAF Northolt two months later. By the following year, some 200 had been delivered and Hawker contracted with the Gloster Aircraft company to produce Hurricanes as well to meet the demand. During production, all-metal wings were added, along with a bullet-proof windscreen, and the engine was upgraded to the Merlin III. Before World War II, production began in Yugoslavia and Belgium, and, in 1940, they began being built in Canada. That summer, alongside the Spitfire, the Hurricane took on the Luftwaffe in the Battle of Britain. Generally Spitfires would take on the German fighters, leaving the Hurricanes to concentrate on destroying the bombers. In that role, the Hurricane scored the highest number of shootdowns, accounting for 1,593 out of the 2,739 total claimed. Later in the war, the Hurricane served in North Africa, Burma, Malta and in nearly every other theatre where the RAF was deployed. During the war, Hurricanes were sold to Egypt, Finland, India, the Irish Air Corps, Persia, Turkey and the Soviet Union.

Below: Hawker Hurricanes on the production line in the run-up to war.

A number of major variants were produced. These included the Mark IIA with a Merlin XX engine; the Mark IIB with interchangeable wings housing 12 0.303-inch guns and carrying two 500 lb bombs; the Mark IID, a tank-buster with two 40-mm anti-tank cannon and two 0.303-inch guns; the Mk IV with a universal, multi-purpose wing and powered by a 1,620-horsepower Merlin 24/27 engine; and the Canadian-built Mark XII, with a 1,300-horsepower Packard Merlin 29 engine. The Hurricane remained in service with the RAF until January 1947.

Mustang

The P-51 Mustang was developed as a fighter escort. The Battle of Britain taught the British that the limited fuel capacity of Messerschmitt 109s left German bombers vulnerable over the target. When Britain decided to retaliate by bombing German cities, it was realized that Bomber Command would be equally vulnerable as Fighter Command's Hurricanes and Spitfires would not be able to escort them far over the Continent. So in April 1940 the British Air Purchasing Commission ordered the P-51 Mustang from North American. Following the attack on Pearl Harbor, America also needed Mustangs, which first took to the air in September 1942. It was quickly found that the aerodynamics of the Mustang were excellent but it was underpowered. Initially fitted with an Allison engine, it was used primarily for photo-reconnaissance. It was then fitted with a V-1650 Merlin engine which gave it sufficient power to use its streamlined shape to full advantage. The Senate War Investigating Committee, set up in 1944, called it "the most aerodynamically perfect pursuit plane in existence".

The Merlin-engined P-51B took to the air in December 1943. In May 1944, the P-51D with fuel drop tanks was introduced, which had far greater range. This allowed the Mustang to escort the US 8th Air Force bombers to just about any target in Western Europe. Mustangs also attacked the Luftwaffe on the ground, destroying many aircraft. As a result the P-51 Mustang had an astonishing kill ratio – 19 enemy planes destroyed for every one Mustang lost. The P-51 Mustang is credited with destroying 4,950 German planes – more than any other Allied fighter. It even downed the jet-powered Me 262s. It was so successful that 55 countries bought Mustangs after World War II had ended.

Right: P-51 Mustangs being prepared for their test flights at North American Aviation's airfield at Inglewood in California.

Above: The Mustang came into its own when fitted with a Merlin engine. It was the only American-built fighter to be flown by the RAF during World War II.

Thunderbolt

Built in greater quantities than any other US fighter, the P-47 Thunderbolt was the heaviest single-engined World War II fighter to go into production, and the first piston-powered fighter to exceed 500 miles per hour. The P-47, known as "the unbreakable" because of its rugged construction and one of America's workhorse fighters of World War II, flew some 546,000 combat sorties between March 1943 and August 1945.

The P-47 began life in 1939 as the AP10, a high-altitude interceptor designed by Alexander Kartveli of the Seversky Airplane Company, which later became Republic Aviation. The new fighter was powered by a 2,000-horsepower turbo-charged Pratt & Whitney radial engine and carried eight .50-calibre machine guns. Production began at Republic's plant in Farmingdale, New York, in July 1942. The first P-47s were delivered to the 56th Fighter Group, stationed only a few miles from the Republic plant, who served as the plane's unofficial test pilots. Eighteen pilots lost their lives before the plane's flaws were ironed out. Christened the Thunderbolt, these early razorback canopy models rolled off the assembly line at a cost of about $85,000 each.

The new P-47s joined the US 8th Air Force in Britain in late 1942, and in August 1943 they were deployed with 348th Fighter Group of the 5th Air Force in the Pacific. Later, extra fuel tanks were added for long-range bomber escort duty. The razorback canopy was replaced by a bubbletop. Bomb racks were installed under the belly and five-inch rocket mounts were added to the wings, changing the P-47 from escort fighter into fighter-bomber.

Major Don Blakeslee recorded the first P-47 kill when he downed a German Fw 190 on 15 April 1943. The top P-47 ace Lieutenant-Colonel Francis S. Gabreski downed 28 enemy planes, while Captain Robert S. Johnson downed 27. More than 15,000 Thunderbolts were produced during World War II.

Right: *The P-47 Thunderbolt was also seen in the skies over Britain in late 1942.*

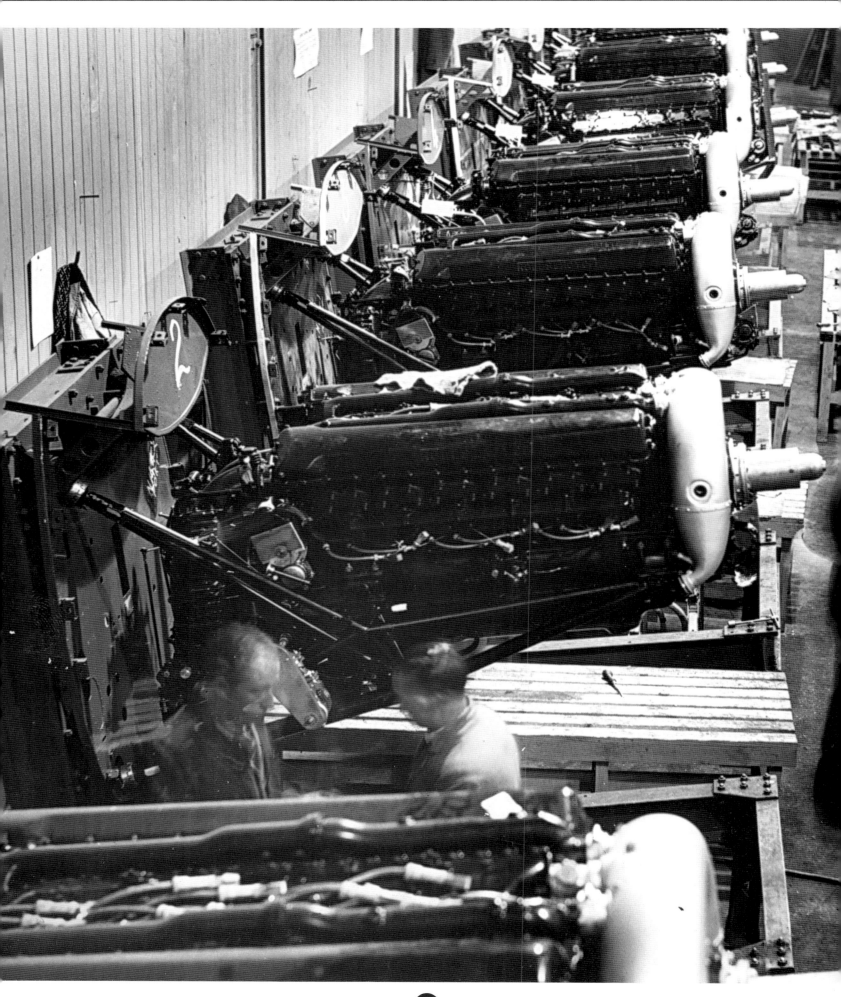

Rolls-Royce Merlin Engine

The development of the Merlin engine was vital to Britain's war effort. It powered not only the Spitfire, but also the Hawker Hurricane, de Havilland Mosquito, Mustang and the Lancaster bomber. The vast majority of Spitfires in the Battle of Britain were fitted with the 1,030-horsepower Merlin III.

By 1932 Rolls-Royce's best-selling engine, the 21.2-litre 745-horsepower Kestrel had reached the end of its development life, so Sir Henry Royce decided to develop a new engine using the experience gained making the Schneider Trophy-winning R engine.

Left: The Rolls-Royce Merlin XX in production. An improved supercharger gave it more power at higher altitudes. Throughout the war, British and American designs continued to improve.

The new engine retained the V12 configuration and geared supercharger of its predecessors, designed to deliver around 1,000 horsepower. The engine was known initially as PV12, as it was a private venture, with development at first entirely funded by Rolls-Royce. In October 1933 the Air Ministry agreed to finance the development and it was renamed Merlin – Rolls-Royce piston engines were by convention named after birds of prey, jets after rivers. Although, in service, the Merlin was known for its reliability, the early development of the engine was plagued with problems, especially with its gear train and cooling system that used ethylene glycol. Later variants used a 30 per cent solution of glycol in water at a pressure of 18 pounds per square inch, which lowered the engine temperature

by 70 degrees centigrade and improved engine life and reliability. In July 1934 the Merlin passed its initial testing, delivering 790 horsepower at 12,000 feet with 2,500 revs per minute. By February 1935, the Merlin B, with a ramp head to the cylinder seen in Rolls-Royce car engines, delivered 950 horsepower at 11,000 feet. The development of the low-profile Merlin C, which delivered 1,000 horsepower, persuaded both R.J. Mitchell and Sydney Camm to base their Spitfire and Hurricane designs around the untried engine. Further modifications produced the Merlin E that delivered 1,045 horsepower and passed a civil 50-hour type test at 955 horsepower. The upgraded Merlin F was released as the Merlin I and the enlarged Merlin G was released as the Merlin II which weighed 1,335 lb and produced 1,030 horsepower and 3,000 revs per minute at 16,250 feet, and ran on 87 octane fuel. In a 1937 attempt to break the World Landplane Speed Record, a specially strengthened Merlin II was used that generated 2,160 horsepower. Most of the modifications developed for this engine eventually found their way into production Merlins from the Merlin III onwards.

Left: *The crank-case bay at a Rolls-Royce aero engine factory. Here the studs that hold the cylinders in place are being fitted.*

Above: *A section through the supercharger of a Merlin I. Rolls-Royce insisted that every component was tested to destruction.*

In 1935 Rolls-Royce added the two-speed Farman supercharger so that it could be run at low speed, using little energy, in the lower altitudes, while being available to enrich the air supply higher up. The first of these engines was the Merlin X. However, the supercharger added significantly to the length of the engine.

In 1939 it was decided to use 100 octane fuel in aero engines from the US. This fuel permitted higher boost pressures and temperatures, allowing the use of +12 lb boost, over the previous limit of +6 lb, for five minutes. With pilots able to call on 1,305 horsepower at 9,000 feet, the rate of climb in particular was increased, enabling numerous lone Spitfires to escape dangerous situations. It also proved useful during an attack.

Left: *A Merlin II ready to be fitted to any aircraft that would help Britain win the war.*

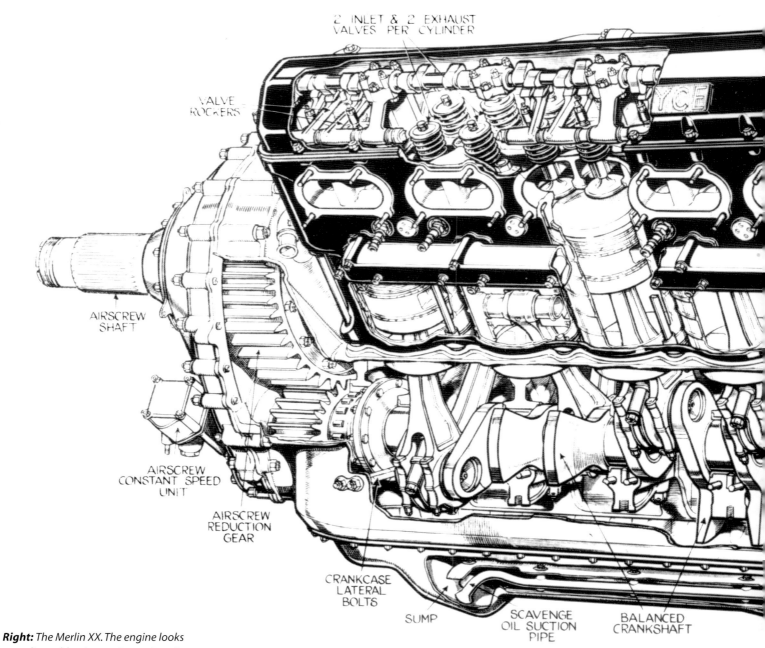

2 INLET & 2 EXHAUST
VALVES PER CYLINDER

VALVE
ROCKERS

AIRSCREW
SHAFT

AIRSCREW
CONSTANT SPEED
UNIT

AIRSCREW
REDUCTION
GEAR

CRANKCASE
LATERAL
BOLTS

SUMP

SCAVENGE
OIL SUCTION
PIPE

BALANCED
CRANKSHAFT

Right: The Merlin XX. The engine looks
complicated, but its precise engineering
made it tremendously reliable.

The Merlin XII, with a higher supercharger gearing, providing up to 12.5 lb boost, and a
Coffman cartridge starter, marked the difference between the Spitfire I and II. Further
modifications of the supercharger produced the Merlin XX, which gave more power at much
higher altitudes – 1,175 horsepower at 20,000 feet compared to 1,160 horsepower at 13,500
feet for the Merlin II. This was used in the Spitfire Mark V.

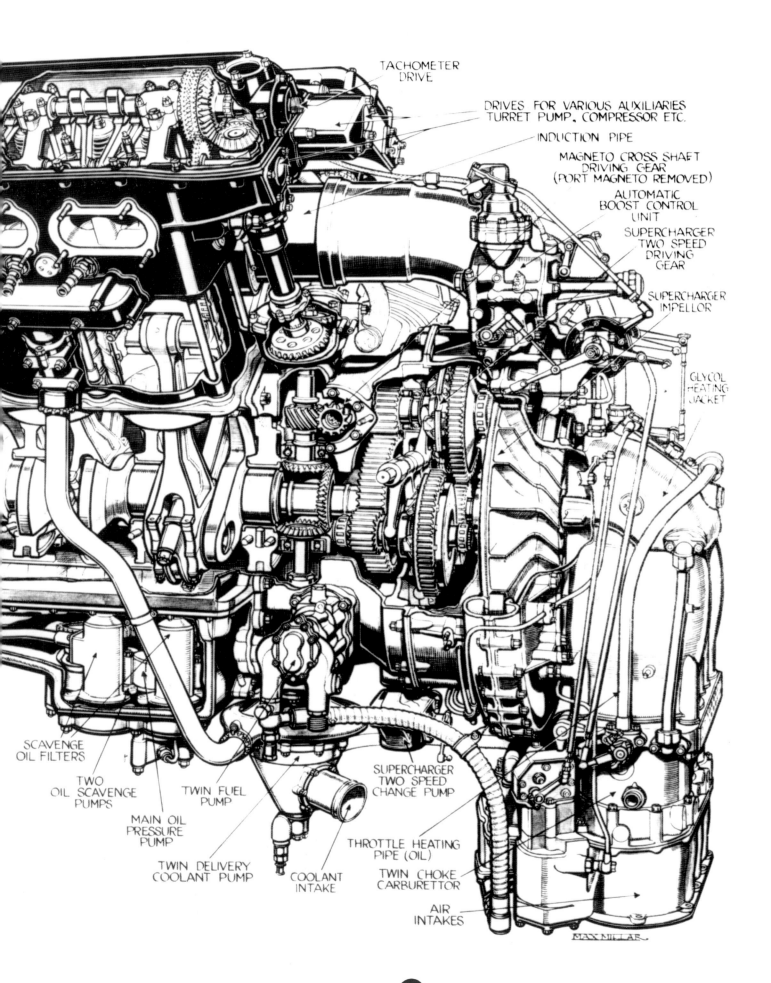

TACHOMETER
DRIVE

DRIVES FOR VARIOUS AUXILIARIES
TURRET PUMP, COMPRESSOR ETC.

INDUCTION PIPE

MAGNETO CROSS SHAFT
DRIVING GEAR
(PORT MAGNETO REMOVED)

AUTOMATIC
BOOST CONTROL
UNIT

SUPERCHARGER
TWO SPEED
DRIVING
GEAR

SUPERCHARGER
IMPELLOR

GLYCOL
HEATING
JACKET

SCAVENGE
OIL FILTERS

TWO
OIL SCAVENGE
PUMPS

MAIN OIL
PRESSURE
PUMP

TWIN FUEL
PUMP

TWIN DELIVERY
COOLANT PUMP

COOLANT
INTAKE

SUPERCHARGER
TWO SPEED
CHANGE PUMP

THROTTLE HEATING
PIPE (OIL)

TWIN CHOKE
CARBURETTOR

AIR
INTAKES

MAX MILLAR

Other engines were modified to give maximum power at low altitudes, since most of the air combat was taking place around 6,000 feet.

The development of high-altitude bombers required the development of an engine with a higher full-throttle height. Rather than move to turbochargers, it was decided to use two superchargers in series. Since a high-altitude supercharger of the right size had already been developed, the output from the Rolls-Royce Vulture supercharger was simply fed into the supercharger of a Merlin 46. The only modification required was the incorporation of a cooling stage after the two supercharger stages. The new engine had a full-throttle height of nearly 30,000 feet. Although intended for the Mark VIII, it was possible to fit the engine to the Spitfire Mark V airframe, producing the Spitfire Mark IX/XVI series. The extra cooling was provided by an enlarged radiator under the left wing.

As the power increased, the design work focused on strengthening. An engine was run at high power until something broke, then that part was strengthened or redesigned and the process repeated. As a result a Merlin engine was developed that could produce 2,030 horsepower at low level and 1,000 horsepower at up to 36,000 feet. By late 1944 a Merlin was run for 15 minutes at 2,640 horsepower. It seemed that Merlins could withstand any amount of abuse. It was one of the few engines that could tolerate full power loads for long periods. There are records of Lancaster pilots losing one of their four Merlins shortly after take-off, but simply continuing the mission with all the remaining throttles pushed to the limit. However, the engines rarely failed.

The Merlin was also produced under licence in the US by Packard. These engines were used in the Spitfire XVI. Then they were used in the P-51 Mustang, transforming it from a low-altitude army co-operation fighter into the long-range, high-altitude nemesis of the Luftwaffe.

After World War II, 500, 600 and 700 series Merlins were developed for civilian transports, though the jet engine gradually took over. In all, 168,040 Merlin engines were made.

Below: *The Packard version of the Merlin engine, built under licence in the US.*

PLEASE DO NOT TOUCH THE EXHIBITS

Carburettor Design

The Merlin engine used a carburettor, rather than the fuel injection seen on German planes. Consequently, it tended to cut out under negative G force. Luftwaffe pilots learned to escape a pursuing Spitfire by simply pushing the nose of their aircraft down into a dive, pulling negative G. The Spitfire would fall behind until the engine picked up again. It only took a second or two, but that was all the German needed to escape. Spitfire pilots developed a way around this by doing a half-roll before the dive. This meant that the G force acted in the opposite direction and the Merlin was unaffected. By 1941 the engineer Tilly Shilling in Farnborough had developed a partial cure for the problem. This involved a diaphragm across the float chambers with a calibrated hole – known, rudely, as "Miss Shilling's orifice" – which allowed the engine to continue for short periods of negative G. It was fitted as standard from March 1941. After 1942 a series of fully negative-G carburettors were added.

It should also be remembered that the Merlin engine was smaller than its rivals – just 27 litres, compared to the Messerschmitt's 39-litre CB601 and the Focke-Wulf 42-litre BMW801. Nevertheless, the performance of later Merlins in particular was superior.

Below: A section through a Merlin engine built in 1943.

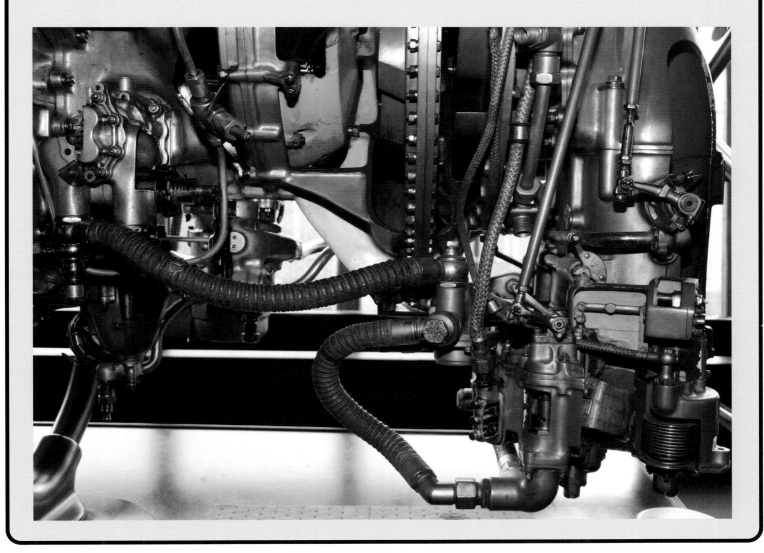

Specifications for the Merlin II/III

Design

Type: 12-cylinder supercharged liquid-cooled 60-degree "V" piston aero engine

Bore: 5.4 inches (137.2 mm)

Stroke: 6 inches (152.4 mm)

Displacement: 1,648.96 cubic inches (27.04 litres)

Length: 69 inches (175.3 cm)

Width: 29.8 inches (75.7 cm)

Height: 41.2 inches (104.6 cm)

Weight: 1,375 lb (623.7 kg)

Components

Valve train: Overhead camshaft-actuated, two intake and two exhaust valves per cylinder, sodium-cooled exhaust valve stems

Supercharger: Single stage, single speed

Fuel system: Twin-choke updraft carburettor with automatic mixture control

Fuel type: 87, later 100, octane aviation fuel

Oil system: Dry sump with one pressure pump and two scavenge pumps

Cooling system: 100 per cent ethylene glycol, pressurized

Performance

Power output: (Maximum boost pressures 87 octane +6.25 lb; 100 octane fuel +9 lb)

880 horsepower (656 kW) at 3,000 revs per minute at take-off

1,030 horsepower (768 kW) at 3,000 revs per minute at 16,000 feet (4,877 m) (+6.25 lb)

1,160 horsepower (865 kW) at 3,000 revs per minute at 12,250 feet (3,734 m) (+9 lb)

Specific power: 0.70 horsepower per cubic inch (42.9 kW/litre)

Compression ratio: 6:1

Power-to-weight ratio: 0.844 horsepower per lb (1.86 kW/kg)

Specifications for the Merlin 66

Design

Type: 12-cylinder supercharged liquid-cooled 60-degree "V" piston aero engine

Bore: 5.4 inches (137.2 mm)

Stroke: 6 inches (152.4 mm)

Displacement: 1,648.96 cubic inches (27.04 litres)

Length: 88.7 inches (225.3 cm)

Width: 30.8 inches (78.1 cm)

Height: 40 inches (101.6 cm)

Dry weight: 1,645 lb (746.5 kg)

Components

Valve train: Overhead camshaft-actuated, two intake and two exhaust valves per cylinder, sodium-cooled exhaust valve stems

Supercharger: Two-speed, two-stage, boost pressure automatically linked to the throttle, water-air after-cooler installed between the second stage and the engine

Fuel system: Twin-choke updraft carburettor with automatic mixture control

Fuel type: 100 octane, from mid-1944 100/150 grade aviation fuel

Oil system: Dry sump with one pressure pump and two scavenge pumps

Cooling system: 30 per cent ethylene glycol, 70 per cent water coolant mixture, pressurized

Performance

Power output:

(100 octane fuel, +12 lb boost)

1,315 horsepower (981 kW) at 3,000 revs per minute at take-off

1,705 horsepower (1,271 kW) at 3,000 revs per minute at 5,750 feet (1,753 m) (MS gear)

1,580 horsepower (1,178 kW) at 3,000 revs per minute at 16,000 feet (4,877 m) (FS gear)

(100/150 Grade fuel, +25 lb boost)

2,000 horsepower (1,491 kW) at 5,250 feet (1,600 m) (MS gear)

1,860 horsepower (1,387 kW) at 11,000 feet (3,353 m) (FS gear)

Specific power: 0.95 horsepower per cubic inch (43.3 kW/litre)

Compression ratio: 6:1

Power-to-weight ratio: 0.80 horsepower per lb (1.76 kW/kg) take-off; 1.21 horsepower per lb (2.69 kW/kg) 100/150 grade fuel/MS gear

The Spitfire's specifications versus the Hawker Hurricane, the Messerschmitt Bf 109 and the North American P-51 Mustang.

Spitfire Mk Vb

General

Crew: one pilot

Length: 29 feet 11 inches (9.12 m)

Wingspan: 36 feet 10 inches (11.23 m)

Height: 11 feet 5 inches (3.86 m)

Wing area: 242.1 square feet (22.48 m²)

Aerofoil: NACA 2200

Empty weight: 5,090 lb (2,309 kg)

Loaded weight: 6,622 lb (3,000 kg)

Maximum takeoff weight: 6,770 lb (3,071 kg)

Powerplant: 1x Rolls-Royce Merlin 45 supercharged V12 engine, 1,470 horsepower at 9,250 feet (1,096 kW at 2,820 m)

Performance

Maximum speed: 378 mph, (330 knots, 605km/h)

Combat radius: 410 nmi (470 mi, 760 km)

Ferry range: 991 nmi (1,140 mi, 1,840 km)

Service ceiling 35,000 feet (10,668 m)

Rate of climb: 2,665 feet a minute (13.5 m/s)

Wing loading: 24.56 lb per square foot (119.91 kg/m²)

Power/mass: 0.22 horsepower per lb (360 W/kg)

Armament

Guns: Mk I, Mk II, Mk VA

8x 0.303-inch (7.7-mm) Browning machine guns, 350 rounds per gun

Later versions (VB on):

2x 20-mm (0.787-inch) Hispano Mark II cannon, 60 (later 120 – Mark Vc) shells per gun

4x 0.303-inch (7.7-mm) Browning machine guns, 350 rounds per gun

Bombs: 2x 250 lb (110 kg) bombs

Hurricane IIC

General

Crew: One

Length: 32 feet 3 inch (9.84 m)

Wingspan: 40 feet (12.19 m)

Height: 13 feet 1 inch (4 m)

Wing area: 257.5 square feet (23.92 m²)

Empty weight: 5,745 lb (2,605 kg)

Loaded weight: 7,670 lb (3,480 kg)

Max takeoff weight: 8,710 lb (3,950 kg)

Powerplant: 1x Rolls-Royce Merlin XX liquid-cooled V-12, 1,185 horsepower at 21,000 feet (883 kW at 6,400 m)

Performance

Maximum speed: 340 mph (54 km/h) at 21,000 feet (6,400 m) (320 mph (514 km/h) at 19,700 feet (6,004 m) with two 250 lb bombs)

Range: 600 miles (965 km)

Service ceiling: 36,000 feet (10,970 m)

Rate of climb: 2,780 feet a minute (14.1 m/s)

Wing loading: 29.8 lb per square foot (121.9 kg/m²)

Power/mass: 6.47 lb power horsepower (3.94 kg/kW)

Armament

Guns: IIa: 8x 0.303-inch (7.7mm) Browning machine guns

IIb: 12x 0.303-inch (7.7mm) Browning machine guns

IIc: 4x 20mm Hispano Mark II cannon

IId: 2x 40mm Vickers Type S cannon, 2x 0.303-inch (7.7mm) Browning machine guns

Bombs (Mark IIb and later models): 2x 250 lb or 500 lb bombs

Messerschmitt Bf 109 G-6

General

Crew: One

Length: 8.95 m (29 feet 7 inch)

Wingspan: 9.925 m (32 feet 6 inch)

Height: 2.60 m (8 feet 2 inch)

Wing area: 16.40 m (173.3 square feet)

Empty weight: 2,247 kg (4,954 lb)

Loaded weight: 3,148 kg (6,940 lb)

Max takeoff weight: 3,400 kg (7,495 lb)

Powerplant: 1x Daimler-Benz DB 605A-1 liquid-cooled inverted V12, 1,475 PS (1,455 horsepower, 1,085kW)

Performance

Maximum speed: 640 km/h (398 mph) at 6,300m (20,669 feet)

Cruise speed: 590 km/h (365 mph) at 6,000m (19,680 feet)

Range: 850km (528 miles) with droptank 1,000km (620 miles)

Service ceiling: 12,000 m (39,370 feet)

Rate of climb: 17.0m/s (3,345 feet per minute)

Wing loading: 199.8 kg/m² (40.9 lb per square foot)

Power/mass: 330 W/kg (0.21 horsepower per lb)

Armament

2x 13-mm MG 131 machine guns with 500 rounds per gun

1x 20-mm MG 151/20 cannon (or 1x 30-mm Mark 108, G-6/U4)

1x 250 kg (550 lb) bomb or 4x50 kg (110 lb) bombs or (1x300 l (78 US gal) drop tank)

2x WGr.21 rockets (G-6 with BR21)

2x 20-mm MG 151/20 underwing cannon pods with 200 rounds per gun (G-6 with R6)

North American P-51D Mustang

General

Crew: One

Length: 32 feet 3 inches (9.83 m)

Wingspan: 37 feet (11.28 m)

Height: 13 feet 8 inches (4.17 m)

Wing area: 235 square feet (21.83 m)

Empty weight: 7,635 lb (3,465 kg)

Loaded weight: 9,200 lb (4,175 kg)

Max takeoff weight: 12,100 lb (5,490 kg)

Powerplant: 1x Packard Merlin V-1650-7 liquid-cooled supercharged V-12, 1,695 horsepower (1,265 kW)

Zero-lift drag coefficient: 0.0163

Drag area: 3.80 square feet (0.35 m²)

Aspect ratio: 5.83

Performance

Maximum speed: 437 mph (703 km/h) at 25,000 feet (7,620 m)

Cruise speed: 362 mph (580 km/h)

Stall speed: 100 mph (160 km/h)

Range: 1,650 miles (2,755 km) with external tanks

Service ceiling: 41,900 feet (12,770 m)

Rate of climb: 3,200 feet a minute (16.3 m/s)

Wing loading: 39 lb per square foot (192 kg/m²)

Power/mass: 0.18 horsepower per lb (300 W/kg)

Lift-to-drag ratio: 14.6

Recommended Mach limit: 0.8

Armament

6 x 0.50-inch (12.7-mm) machine guns; 400 rounds per gun for the two inboard guns; 270 per outboard gun

2 hardpoints for up to 2,000 lb (907 kg)

10 x 5-inch (127-mm) rockets

Chapter 6

Construction

Structurally, the Spitfire was straightforward. It was one of a new generation of all-metal, low-wing fighter aircraft, such as the Messerschmitt Bf 109 and the French Dewoitine D520, that were designed to take advantage of new techniques of monocoque construction, and new high-powered, liquid-cooled aero engines. They also featured refinements such as a retractable undercarriage, fully enclosed cockpits and low-drag, all-metal wings. These had all been introduced on US civil airliners some time earlier, but the military had continued to favour the simplicity and manoeuvrability of the biplane.

Above: *The Messerschmitt Bf 109 and the Spitfire shared many common features.*

Above: *The two planes were so similar that it was possible to swap engines.*

Below: The Messerschmitt Bf 109's all-metal, low wing monocoque construction came from the same generation of design as the Spitfire.

Dewoitine D520

After a number of other prototypes and proposals had been rejected, French aeroplane designer Emile Dewoitine decided that his Dewoitine D520 fighter would gain government approval once the military saw it fly. The first prototype D520.01 flew in October 1938, and featured a Hispano-Suiza 12Y-21 V engine cooled with ethylene glycol. Its top speed was only a disappointing 301 miles per hour, partly because of the fixed-pitch type wooden two-blade propeller and the two underwing radiators. When a metal three-blade propeller, a central radiator and a Hispano-Suiza 12Y-29 engine were added, the top speed rose to 332 miles per hour. It carried a 20-mm cannon firing through the propeller, and four 7.5-mm machine guns in the wings.

The first order for 200 aircraft was placed in April 1939, quickly followed by further orders. But production was slow. Only 36 were delivered when Germany invaded in May 1940. By the time France capitulated on 25 June, 437 had been produced of which 403 had been delivered.

The D520 was slower but more manoeuvrable than the Messerschmitt Bf 109E. The five D520 units scored 108 confirmed victories and 39 probable victories. The confirmed victories included 23 Bf 109s and 9 Bf 110s. In the same period 106 D520s were lost, although only 26 in air-to-air combat. If the D520 had been available in larger numbers, it may well have denied the Luftwaffe control of the air over the Western Front.

After the defeat of France, production of the D520 continued. They saw action at the hands of both the Vichy government and the Free French. Germany used a number of D520s for training, and operationally on the Eastern Front. Bulgaria had 120 D520s which it flew, first on the German side, then on the Allied side. Italy's 60 D520s were used as home defence fighters.

Below: The Dewoitine D520 put up a creditable performance against the Messerschmitt Bf 109.

The Spitfire's design combined a light alloy monocoque fuselage and a single spar wing with stressed skin covering and, initially, fabric-covered control surfaces. To preserve the clean nose cowling lines originally conceived by R.J. Mitchell, the radiator was located beneath the starboard wing with the smaller oil cooler beneath the port wing causing some asymmetry. The air intake for the carburettor was under the centre fuselage.

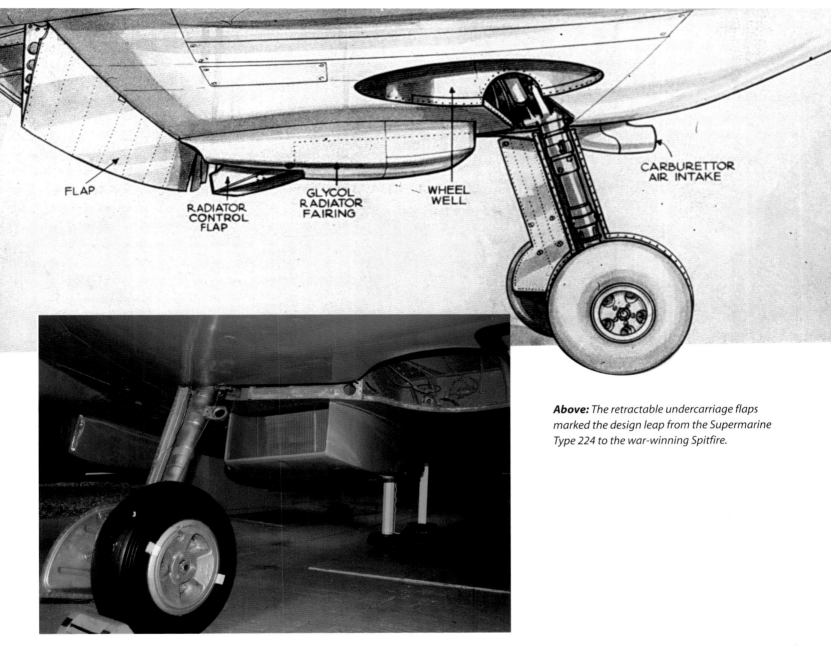

FLAP

RADIATOR CONTROL FLAP

GLYCOL RADIATOR FAIRING

WHEEL WELL

CARBURETTOR AIR INTAKE

Above: *The retractable undercarriage flaps marked the design leap from the Supermarine Type 224 to the war-winning Spitfire.*

Above: *The trademark elliptical wing left plenty of room to stow the undercarriage.*

Monocoque

Monocoque means "single shell" in French. It is a construction technique where the load is borne by the external skin rather than an internal frame or chassis. Early aircraft were built on an internal frame, typically of wood or steel tubing, which was then covered with fabric to give it a smooth surface. Some aircraft builders began using plywood or sheet metal for the skin, but the internal load-bearing structure remained.

In 1916 Luft-Fahrzeug-Gesellschaft, a World War I German aircraft manufacturer, began using a fuselage made of moulded plywood that formed the main load-bearing structure as well as the external skin. This made the plane extremely strong compared with contemporary designs, although it also made it heavy. Then in the late 1920s the price of aluminium – specifically duralumin, the age-hardened alloy used in aircraft manufacture – started dropping considerably and manufacturers started using it to replace the internal framing, in some, the external skin. The strength and lightness of duralumin made it possible to combine the load-bearing structure and the skin in modern monocoque designs.

Caption

A de Havilland wooden fixed-pitch propeller was used on the prototype and the first Spitfire Is had the Airscrew Company's wooden fixed pitch. Later, a de Havilland three-blade, two-position propeller was adopted after trials on the first prototype. The new propeller gave a five miles per hour increase in speed. In 1940, de Havilland three-blade constant speed propellers were substituted. The first production Spitfires had a fixed tail wheel and triple ejector exhaust manifolds. The X80 HP Rolls-Royce Merlin II and later the Merlin III engine was installed.

Mitchell's design aims were to create a well-balanced high-performance fighter aircraft which would be able to fully utilize the power of the Merlin engine and, at the same time, would be relatively easy to fly. To that end his design team developed an airframe which, for its day, was complex. The streamlined duralumin fuselage featured a large number of compound curves and was built up from a skeleton of 19 frames. These started with frame number one which was the main engine bulkhead.

Left: *With men away fighting the war, many women were employed in war work. Here Anne Godfrey assembles the pilot's control rods, completing the engine. It is now ready for the test bed.*

Below: *Later in the war, some Spitfires were fitted with Rolls-Royce Griffon engines. This made them faster, but limited their range, so they were largely used for home defence.*

Duralumin

Duralumin is a strong, hard, lightweight aluminium alloy widely used in the aircraft industry. Typically it contains 3 to 4 per cent copper, 0.5 to 1.5 per cent magnesium and 0.5 to 1 per cent manganese. Sometimes silicon is added. It was developed and patented by the German metallurgist Alfred Wilm in Düren, Germany, in 1910, after Wilm discovered that after quenching, an aluminium alloy containing a trace of copper would slowly harden when left at room temperature for several days; in its normal state, aluminium remains ductile and easy to work. It was first used in rigid airship frames and its composition and heat treatment remained a secret during World War I. The use of duralumin quickly spread throughout the aircraft industry in the early 1930s, where it was well suited to the new monocoque construction that was being introduced at the same time. Because duralumin loses strength during welding, a special laminated sheet called alclad is used to make aircraft. It had a skin of pure aluminium to prevent corrosion over the strong duralumin core. Zemaitis Guitars use carved duralumin tops on their Metal Top line of guitars.

AERIAL

PETROL
TANKS

SLIDING
COWL

PARACHUTE
FLARES

RUDDER
TAB

ELEVATOR
TAB

TAIL WHEEL
SHOCK
ABSORBER

BATTERY

UNDERCARRIAGE PUMP HANDLE

WHEEL

MAX
MILLAR

RETRACTABLE
LANDING
LIGHT

UNDERCARRIAGE
SHOCK ABSORBER
LEG

GLYCOL
COOLING RADIATOR

UNDERCARRIAGE
HYDRAULIC
RAM

Aft of the engine bulkhead were five half-frames that surrounded the fuel tanks and cockpit. The pilot's seat and, later, armour plating, was attached to the seventh frame. From here to frame 15, the frames were oval. Each was slightly smaller than the one in front of it and they had holes drilled in them to lighten the structural weight without weakening it. Frame 15 itself was just forward of the tailfin and mounted at a forward angle. Frame 16 formed a double bulkhead with frame 17, which was extended vertically to form the main spar of the tail fin, with frame 18 forming the secondary spar behind it. Behind that was frame 19 that formed the rudder post. Sheets of alclad stressed skinning were attached to two main longerons and 14 longitudinal stringers formed a light but rigid structure.

The skin of the fuselage, wings and tailplane was attached with rivets. In areas where an uninterrupted airflow was required, such as the wing forward of the main spar, flush rivets were used. In less critical areas, such as the rear of the wing, the top was riveted and, at first, the bottom was fixed by woodscrews screwed into sections of spruce. Later, pop-rivets would be used for these areas. Then, from 1943 on, flush riveting was used throughout the entire airframe. The first fully flush-riveted Spitfire was the Mark XII, then all the Mark IXs built at Castle Bromwich.

Early on, the rudder ailerons and elevators were covered with fabric. However, once in combat, it was found that the fabric-covered ailerons did not work at high speeds, and they were replaced by ailerons built in a light alloy. This gave better control throughout the Spitfire's entire speed range.

It has been suggested that Mitchell copied the Spitfire's trademark elliptical wing shape from the Heinkel He 70. Mitchell's aerodynamicist, Beverly Shenstone, has pointed out, however, that the He70 was designed to fulfil a completely different role. Other aircraft at that time had elliptical wings. Mitchell and the Günther brothers, who designed the Heinkel, were well aware of the efficiency of this wing shape.

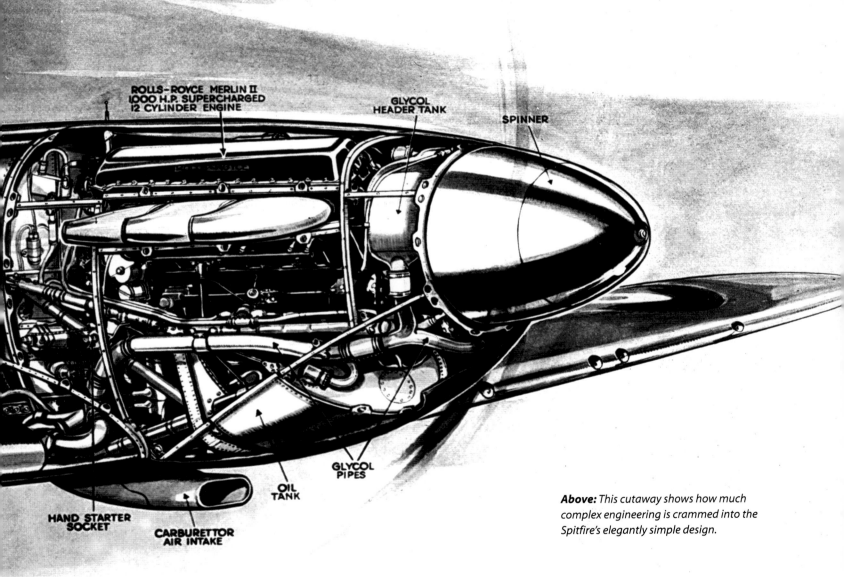

ROLLS-ROYCE MERLIN II
1000 H.P. SUPERCHARGED
12 CYLINDER ENGINE

GLYCOL
HEADER TANK

SPINNER

GLYCOL
PIPES

OIL
TANK

HAND STARTER
SOCKET

CARBURETTOR
AIR INTAKE

Above: This cutaway shows how much complex engineering is crammed into the Spitfire's elegantly simple design.

Heinkel He 70

The Heinkel He 70 Blitz started life as a fast mailplane for Luft Hansa. It was a monoplane that featured a low elliptical wing, which Siegfried and Walter Günther had already used in the Bäumer Sausewind sports plane they designed before they joined Heinkel. To minimize drag it used countersunk rivets to give a smooth surface finish, and was powered by a BMW VI V-12 engine, cooled by ethylene glycol, allowing a smaller radiator. It also had a retractable undercarriage, a novel feature for a German aircraft. The pilot and radio operator were seated in tandem. A cabin carried four passengers on two double seats facing each other. It first flew in 1932. With a top speed of 222 miles per hour, it soon set eight world records for speed over distance.

Lufthansa used He 70s between 1933 and 1937 for fast domestic flights. In 1937, the remaining aircraft were transferred to the Luftwaffe. However, the airframe was made out of a light, yet strong alloy of magnesium, which burns spontaneously in air when heated. A single hit from a light machine gun would set the entire plane alight, killing the crew. While the He 70 saw only limited service as a trainer during World War II, it was the antecedent of the famous Heinkel He 111, which was the major bomber type in the early years of the war, and the Heinkel He 112 fighter. The He 70 was exported to Japan where it inspired the Aichi D3A (Val) carrier-launched light bomber, used in the attack on Pearl Harbor.

It is also commonly believed to be an inspiration or influence for the Supermarine Spitfire's elliptical wing, as an He 70 was used as a test aircraft for the Rolls-Royce Kestrel engine in England at the time of the Spitfire's development.

Below: *The Heinkel He 7 Blitz won eight world speed records before it became a bomber with the Condor Legion in the Spanish Civil War.*

However, the Spitfire's wing was much thinner than that of the Heinkel and had a completely different section. For Mitchell it was the perfect design solution, giving the wing the lowest possible thickness-to-chord ratio to reduce drag, while having room to install a retractable undercarriage, as well as carrying guns and ammunition – especially when, in April 1935, the requirement was changed from two .303-inch Vickers machine guns in each wing to four .303 Brownings. It was the single-spar elliptical wing that sold the new Type 300 to the Air Ministry.

The wing was constructed around an innovative spar boom, made up of five square concentric tubes which fitted into each other. Two of these booms were linked together by an alloy web creating a lightweight and very strong main spar. The undercarriage legs were attached to pivot points built into the main spar and retracted outwards and slightly backwards into wells in the non-load-bearing wing structure.

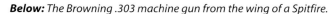

Below: *The Browning .303 machine gun from the wing of a Spitfire.*

This meant that the wheels were not far apart, giving the undercarriage a narrow track. It also meant that the impact of landing was transmitted to the strongest parts of the wing structure. The elliptical wing was able to reach a safe Mach number of 0.83 and maximum of 0.86 without encountering the problem of Mach-induced aileron flutter, a phenomenon that continued to cause problems in later designs.

Ahead of the spar, the thick-skinned leading edge of the wing formed a strong and very rigid D-shaped box, which was originally designed as a condenser tank for the Goshawk engine's cooling system. This took most of the wing load. The wing section used was a NACA 2200 series. This comes from a system of aerofoil classification established by America's National Advisory Committee for Aeronautics, set up during World War I to promote aeronautical research. It became NASA in 1958. The numbers following specify the camber, chord and thickness of the wing. In the Spitfire, NACA 2200 had been adapted to create a thickness-to-chord ratio of 13 per cent at the root, reducing to 6 per cent at the tip. A dihedral, or the angle the wing is inclined above the horizontal, of six degrees was adopted to give increased lateral stability.

Another feature of the wing was its washout. The trailing edge of the wing twisted slightly upward along its span, the angle of incidence decreased from +2 degrees at its root to -1/2 degree at its tip. This caused the wing roots to stall before the tips, reducing tip stall that may have resulted in a spin. In a tight turn the disturbance of the slipstream near the wing-root caused a distinctive "juddering" through the control column and fuselage skin, warning the pilot that the plane was about to stall. Many other aircraft of the time gave no advance warning and would flick straight into a spin, which was often fatal. In combat, experienced pilots were able to use the tight turning ability and stall warning provided by the wing to full advantage, while a Messerschmitt Bf 109, with its higher stalling speed, could often fall into a spin without much warning.

Right: The undercarriage retracts to give the Spitfire its clean aerodynamic shape.

At first the complexity of the wing design, especially the precision required to manufacture the vital spar and leading edge structures, caused some major hold-ups in the production of the Spitfire. This also caused complications when the work was put out to subcontractors, who had never dealt with metal-structured, high-speed aircraft. Gradually these problems were overcome as thousands of wings in six basic types were manufactured.

One flaw in the thin-wing design of the Spitfire manifested itself when the aircraft was brought up to very high speeds. When the pilot attempted to roll the aircraft at these speeds, the aerodynamic forces on the ailerons were enough to twist the entire wing-tip. This produced "aileron reversal", with the Spitfire rolling in the opposite direction to the control-column input. The new wing of the Spitfire F Mark 21, introduced in 1943, and its successors pushed the theoretical aileron reversal speed from 580 to 850 miles per hour.

The Spitfire's fin and tailplanes again exploited the favourable aerodynamic characteristics of the ellipse. Both the elevators and rudder were shaped so that their centre of mass was shifted forward reducing control surface flutter. The longer noses and greater propeller wash resulting from larger engines used in later models meant that larger vertical and horizontal surfaces in the tail assembly were needed to compensate – those of the Mark 22/24 series which were 25 per cent larger in area than those of the Mark I.

Above: *The Mk IX was produced to counter the FW190. As a matter of urgency the Mk Vc airframe was married to the new Merlin 61 engine with a two-speed supercharger. Note also the clipped wings on this aircraft.*

Above: *In flight, the Spitfire was effortlessly manoeuvrable.*

Chapter 7
Production

The prototype Spitfire, K5054, first flew on 6 March 1936, from Eastleigh Aerodrome. Testing continued until 26 May 1936, when it was flown to RAF Martlesham Heath and handed over to Squadron Leader Anderson of the Aeroplane & Armament Experimental Establishment. They were so impressed that the Air Ministry placed an order for 310 aircraft on 3 June 1936, before any formal report had been issued by the A&AEE, and it first went on show to the public at the RAF Hendon air-display on Saturday 27 June 1936. The problem was that Supermarine's Woolston factory was too small to produce planes in any number. Consequently, they began one of the largest subcontracting schemes ever undertaken in Britain.

Left: *The first sight of the prototype led to an Air Ministry order for 310 planes.*

Below: *After the Hendon air display, the prototype Spitfire went on display at Brooklands on 30 June 1936.*

Spitfire production deliveries began in June 1938, two years after the first production contract had been placed, and they entered service with 19 Squadron on 4 August. On 29 April the following year, contracts were placed with Supermarine for a further 200 Spitfires and on 9 August for another 450. But with Hitler gearing for war, it became apparent that, even with subcontracting, a single factory was not going to be able to satisfy the demand.

Above: *The instrumentation in the Spitfire's cockpit appears rudimentary, though it was sophisticated for its day.*

Above: *The Spitfire I, P9450, photographed during April 1940, has the production standard and markings of the period. The most noticeable features are the tapered aerial mast, which replaced the earlier 'stick' type, and the addition of an external armoured windscreen. This aircraft went to 64 Squadron at Kenley but was damaged during the Battle of Britain, after which it was converted to a Mark VA.*

During 1937, plans had been made for a "shadow" production line to be established in Castle Bromwich near Birmingham. It was to be equipped by Morris Motors under Lord Nuffield, one of the pioneers of the mass production of motor cars in the UK. On 12 April 1938 a contract was placed for 1,000 Spitfires to be built at this new factory, though work on its construction did not begin until 12 July. The new factory had been completed in late 1939, but they were still having problems in building an airframe. The Spitfire's stressed-skin monocoque construction required skills and techniques beyond the experience of the local motor workers. This problem was exacerbated by the constant stream of changes which were demanded by the RAF.

Above: One of the first production-line Spitfires on test at Eastleigh with Jeffrey Quill at the controls. Jack Brown operates the electric starter while apprentice Frank Wherley waits at the wingtip.

Right: Prime Minister Winston Churchill visits Castle Bromwich to see Spitfires being made.

Castle Bromwich

In 1915, an airfield was established at Berwood Playing Fields. It was a training centre where new aircraft were tried out. It became the home base of 10 Squadron of the Royal Flying Corps. After World War I, it was home to the Midland Aero Club and a refuelling stop on air races. It also became the airport for the first London–Birmingham passenger service. In 1926, 605 Squadron of the Auxiliary Air Force moved in. Then in World War II it became the home of Spitfire production and Alex Henshaw tested Spitfires from the airfield.

Once production got underway, it soon reached 30 Spitfires a week. In May 1942 a further 2,990 Spitfires were ordered – in the largest single order for any British military aircraft. They were the backbone of the Spitfire Squadrons in the last two years of the war. When the factory closed in December 1945, it had built 15,634 Spitfires, including 50 Seafires, and had also made 305 Lancaster bombers, the first of which was completed in late 1943.

On 3 September 1939, when Britain went to war, a total of 2,160 Spitfires were on order, but not a single plane had emerged from Castle Bromwich. On 17 May 1940 – still without a single Spitfire being built – the government took over the Castle Bromwich factory. Lord Beaverbrook, Minister of Aircraft Production, immediately sent in new management and experienced workers from Supermarine and Vickers-Armstrong, and in June, 10 Mark II Spitfires – the first of thousands of Spitfires – emerged from Castle Bromwich.

Right: *The Supermarine premises at Woolston in Southampton, first home of the Spitfire.*

By then the Germans were fully aware of the importance of the Spitfire and during the Battle of Britain the Luftwaffe made concerted efforts to destroy the main factories at Woolston and Itchen, near Southampton. The first raid came on 23 August. It missed the factories, but over the next month other raids were mounted until, on 26 September, both factories were completely wrecked. Some 92 people were killed and a large number injured. Most of the casualties were experienced aircraft production workers.

Fortunately for the future of the Spitfire many of the production jigs and machine tools had already been relocated and steps were being taken to disperse production throughout southern England. Anna Valley Motors in Salisbury became the sole producer of the wing leading-edge fuel tanks for photo-reconnaissance Spitfires, along with other components. Vincent's Garage in Station Square, Reading specialized in manufacturing Spitfire fuselages, and a purpose-built works, specializing in manufacturing fuselages and installing engines, was built at Star Road, Caversham in Reading.

Below: *After Woolston and Itchen had been bombed, Supermarine's production manager Commander James Bird and his team studied large-scale Ordinance Survey maps of Wiltshire, Hampshire and Berkshire to find suitable premises for requisition. Shown here is a sketch map of Spitfire dispersed production.*

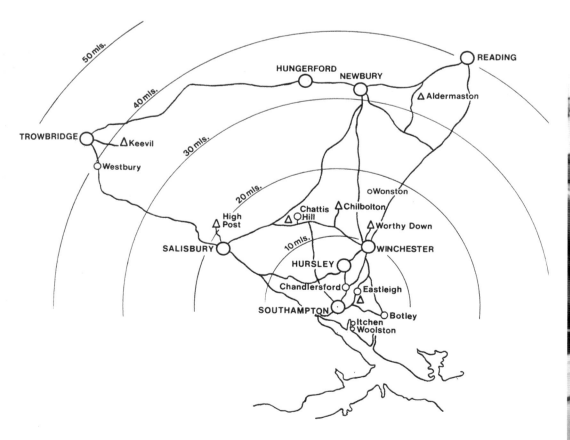

Below: *The machine shop of Shorts in Winchester turning out parts for the Spitfire.*

Below: *Spitfires being assembled at Eastleigh, ready for test flying.*

Above: *The staff at Hursley Park near Southampton where there was a drawing office and facilities to assemble prototypes.*

Right: *Draughtsmen, including women, at work in the drawing office at Hursley Park.*

The drawing office, where Spitfire designs were drafted, was based at another purpose-built site at Hursley Park, near Southampton. The site also had an aircraft assembly hangar, where many of the prototype and experimental Spitfires were assembled. They were tested at the associated aerodrome.

Satellite workshops were set up at Southampton and Eastleigh Airport, in Salisbury around High Post and Chattis Hill aerodromes, at Trowbridge and Keevil aerodrome, and at Reading with Henley and Aldermaston aerodromes. Partially finished Spitfires were delivered to the airfields on large articulated trucks. Then they were fully assembled and tested, before being passed on to the RAF.

Left: *R.J. Mitchell and his drawing-office staff.*

Part of the success of the Spitfire was that every one built was flight tested before it was delivered. Supermarine's test pilot Jeffrey Quill oversaw a group of 10 to 12 pilots who were responsible for testing all developmental and production Spitfires built in the Southampton area. Quill devised the standard testing procedures, which operated from 1938. Alex Henshaw was chief test pilot at Castle Bromwich from 1940. He was in charge of 25 pilots who tested all Spitfires built at that factory. It is estimated that Henshaw flew at least 10 per cent of all Spitfires built.

Right: Test pilots Jeffrey Quill and Dave Morgan compare notes.

Alex Henshaw

The son of a wealthy Lincolnshire family, Alex Henshaw learned to fly at the age of 19 in Skegness. He made a name for himself at 20 competing in the King's Cup races against legendary pilots such as Geoffrey de Havilland, winning the trophy in 1938. He then turned to distance racing, setting a record for a return trip to Cape Town. With the outbreak of World War II, he applied to join Fighter Command, but instead found himself a test pilot at Vickers at Weybridge. He was about to leave to join the RAF's Special Duty Flight, when Jeffrey Quill at Supermarine offered him the job of chief test pilot at Castle Bromwich. As well as testing Spitfires, he flew Hurricanes, Wellingtons and Lancasters, and was the only man known to perform a victory roll in a Lancaster.

After the war he became a director of Miles Aircraft in South Africa, then returned to England to take over the family farming business and wrote a number of books about his experiences. On 5 March 2006, at the age of 91, he took the controls of a Spitfire in a rare two-seater model to celebrate the 70th anniversary of the prototype's first flight. He died at home in Newmarket the following year.

Left: Prime Minister Winston Churchill visits Alex Henshaw, test pilot at Castle Bromwich.

"The Last of the Many".

delivered Dec. 1946.

Aircraft Repaired by AIR SERVICE TRAINING LTD.
From 1940 To 1946.
3507.

A total of 20,351 craft were built, including two-seat trainers. Some remained in service well into the 1950s. The Spitfire was the only British fighter aircraft to be in continual production before, during, and after World War II.

Above: *Damaged Spitfires were too valuable to scrap. If possible, they were repaired and put back into service.*

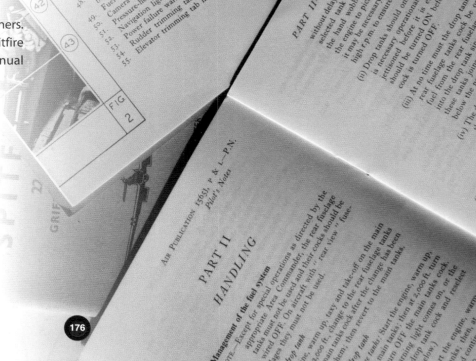

The Cost of a Spitfire in 1940

To support the war effort, the general public was invited to donate the cost of a Spitfire. The aircraft would then bear the name of the donor – an individual, an organization or a town – or any name they proposed in yellow letters four inches high on the side of the fuselage. Lord Beaverbrook set the cost of the airframe at £5,000, although the real cost was nearer £12,000. At the time of the so-called "Spitfire Fund" in the summer of 1940, a price list of the major component parts of a Spitfire was issued by the Air Ministry:

Engine £2,000
Fuselage £2,500
Wings..£1,800
Undercarriage £800
Guns £800
Tail £500
Propeller £350
Petrol tank (top)...£40
Petrol tank (bottom) £25
Oil tank £25
Compass £5
Clock £2 10s 0d (£2.50)
Thermometer £1 1s 0d (£1.05)
Sparking plug 8s 0d (40p)

A further £1,000 could be for a variety of small parts such as screws, cables, switches, sockets, gauges and paint.

The Weight of a Spitfire Mark 1

Fuselage and fin ....426 lb
Engine cowling ....861 lb
Tailplane and elevator...58 lb
Rudder ....18 lb
Wings ....820 lb
Landing gear ....192 lb
Wheels and brakes...90 lb
Seating ....23 lb
Tail wheel...28 lb
Controls ....23 lb
Engine mounting ....58 lb
Engine...1,412 lb
Propeller hub ....36 lb
Propeller..96 lb
Ejector exhausts ....30 lb
Oil tanks ....47 lb
Fuel tanks ....57 lb
Radiator ....98 lb
Cooling system ....56 lb
Glycol (cooling fluid)..142 lb
Engine accessories...61 lb
Guns and ammunition ....685 lb
Petrol (84 gallons)..646 lb
Oil (6 gallons) ....54 lb
Sundries...335 lb

Chapter 8

Service

The first Spitfire to enter service with the RAF arrived at 19 Squadron, Duxford, on 4 August 1938. Over the next few weeks aircraft were delivered at the rate of one a week to both 19 and 66 Squadrons, also based at Duxford. Spitfires then went to 41 Squadron at Catterick, and a number of squadrons stationed at Hornchurch in Essex. The Spitfire first appeared in RAF colours in public on Empire Air Day, 20 May 1939, during a display at Duxford, where the pilot "belly-landed" his aircraft after forgetting to lower his undercarriage. He was consequently fined £5.

Below: A member of the ground crew re-arming Squadron Leader B.J.E. Lane's Spitfire.

Below: The Spitfires of Number 19 Squadron's base at Duxford, Cambridgeshire.

By the outbreak of World War II, the RAF had 306 Spitfires in service, with another 71 in reserve and 2,000 on order. Some 36 had already been written off in accidents. Their first kill occurred on 6 September 1939, when Spitfires of 74 Squadron downed two Hurricanes in a friendly fire incident over the Medway.

First Blood

On 6 September 1939, Spitfires taking off from Hornchurch Airfield in response to an air-raid siren were told that two Hurricanes from North Weald were enemy aeroplanes, and shot them down in an incident known as the Battle of Barking Creek. These two Hurricanes were the first planes shot down by Spitfires. One Hurricane pilot, Frank Rose, survived. The other, Pilot Officer Montague Hulton-Harrop, was the first British pilot to die during World War II. It turned out that the air-raid warning was a false alarm. The two Spitfire pilots, Paddy Byrne and John Freeborn, were cleared by a court martial. John Freeborn, who shot down Pilot Officer Hulton-Harrop, flew more operational hours in the Battle of Britain than any other pilot and was credited with 13½ enemy kills. He was awarded the DFC and bar and ended the war as a Wing Commander.

The Spitfire's action against the enemy took place on 16 October 1939, when six planes from 602 and 603 Squadrons intercepted nine Junkers Ju 88s that were attacking Royal Navy ships in the Firth of Forth. Two Ju 88s were shot down, and another heavily damaged.

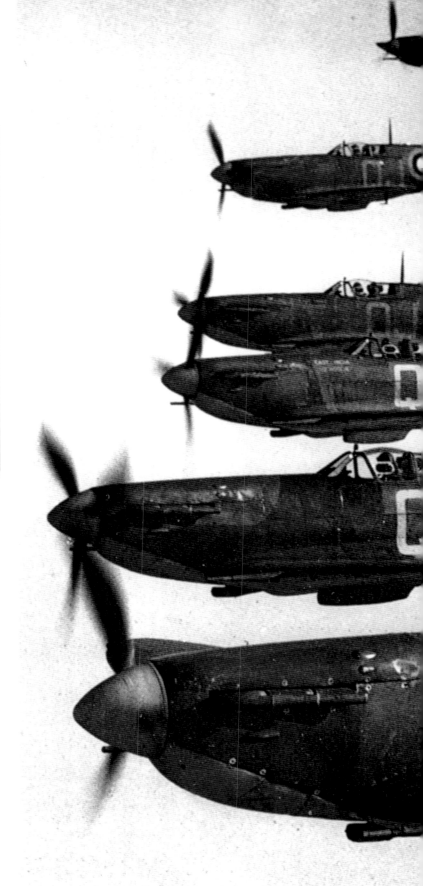

Right: Spitfires of the East India Squadron fitted with 20mm cannon, which proved more effective than machine guns in a dogfight.

Below: *A lucky escape – a pilot smiles; although most of his Spitfire's tail has been shot away, it was still manoeuvrable.*

Above: *Squadron Leader Ratten returns with his Australian squadron after a sweep over the Channel and French coast.*

The first Messerschmitt Bf 109s were shot down by Spitfires of 54 Squadron on 23 May 1940. New Zealand Flying Officer Alan Deere shot down two and Flying Officer "Johnny" Allen downed one. Unwilling to lose Spitfires over France, Air Vice Marshal Hugh Dowding kept Fighter Command in Britain. However, from late 1939, early photo-reconnaissance Spitfires flew from Seclin in northern France to gather valuable photo-intelligence of German defences and cities.

Specification F10/35 dictated that the Spitfire should double as a night fighter. Consequently, Mark Is, IIs, Vas and Vbs were fitted with powerful, retractable landing lights in each wing. Identification lights were fitted on the top just behind the aerial mast and under the belly, which could be operated by a small Morse-key mounted in the cockpit. Also, rectangular light-alloy "blinkers" were fitted to the fuel tank housing to shield the pilot's eyes from the bright exhaust flames. On the night of 18 June, Flight Lieutenant Adolph "Sailor" Malan of 74 Squadron shot down two Heinkel He 111s, while Flying Officers George Ball and John Petre of 19 Squadron each shot down one. Then on the night of 26 June, Flight Lieutenant H. MacDonald of 603 Squadron would down a Heinkel. Pilot Officers R. Smith and R. Marples of 616 Squadron shot down another, while a third was downed by Flying Officers A. Johnstone of 602 Squadron and J. Haig of 603 Squadron, possibly with the help of anti-aircraft guns. Spitfires continued to be used on night patrols, but Luftwaffe bombers then began flying well above the altitudes at which they could be effectively picked up by searchlights.

The Spitfire's greatest moment came in the Battle of Britain, which officially started on 10 July 1940 and ended on 31 October that year. However, the Hurricane downed more fighters and bombers than the Spitfire, mainly because there were more Hurricanes in the air. Seven of every 10 German aircraft shot down during the Battle of Britain were credited to Hurricane pilots, but then more Hurricanes were lost. Post-war analysis showed that the Spitfire's kill ratio was marginally better than the Hurricane's, but the Germans really secured the Spitfire's reputation. Instead of the standard warning of fighter attack – "Achtung, Indianer!" ("Look out, Indians!") – they said "Achtung! Spitfire", even when the attackers were Hurricanes.

Early Spitfires and Hurricanes both carried eight identical .303-inch machine guns. The placement of the Hurricane's guns was better, giving a closer pattern of fire, but its lower top speed and poorer performance at altitude made the Hurricane more vulnerable to German fighter escorts. Wherever possible, Hurricane squadrons were used to attack the bombers, while the Spitfires were held back to take on the escort fighters.

The .303 Browning machine guns on the Mark I and Mark II Spitfires were not particularly effective. It was quite common for German aircraft to return to base with large numbers of .303 bullet holes. The planes were armoured in critical areas and had self-sealing fuel tanks. A smaller number of heavier guns would have been far more effective and 20-mm Hispano-Suiza cannon were progressively fitted.

The Luftwaffe's only comparable plane was the Messerschmitt Bf 109. The Spitfire had the advantage of a higher rate of turn and a smaller turning circle. The pilot also had better visibility through the Spitfire's clear-blown canopy against the Bf 109's heavily framed cockpit canopy. However, initially at least, the Luftwaffe had better tactics.

Right: *The pilot came in a bit low, cropping the blades of his Rotol propeller. But still he managed to land safely back at base.*

In the late 1930s Fighter Command were not expecting to face single-engined fighters over Britain, only bombers. With this in mind they developed "Fighting Area Tactics". They trained to fly in tight, V-shaped sections of three where the pilots were forced to watch each other, rather than to keep an eye out for escort fighters. During the Spanish Civil War, the Luftwaffe had devised a loose section of two. The leader scanned the skies for enemy aircraft, while his wingman, following to starboard and to the rear, concentrated on the leader's blind-spots. Two of these sections were teamed up to form a Schwarm. Because the 109s were well spread, the Schwarm was hard to spot, unlike the RAF V formation. The 109s could attack and defend in pairs, while the RAF formations split into lone aircraft which were vulnerable. Because the loose Schwarm reduced the risk of collision, they were able to climb faster and higher than the tightly grouped RAF fighters, which is one reason why even Spitfire units found themselves being attacked from above.

Some RAF units had "weavers", a single aircraft which flew behind the V formations of main squadrons. The weavers were easily picked off by the German fighters. Often the rest of the squadron did not even know they were under attack.

Below: Test firing the guns at Digby, Lincolnshire.

POLISH AIR FORCE
FIGHTER SQDNS
302
~CITY OF POZNAŃ~
303
~KOŚCIUSZKO~
306
~CITY OF TORUŃ~
307
~CITY OF LWÓW~
308
~CITY OF KRAKÓW~
309
OF PROVINCE
~ZIEMIA CZERWIENSKA~
315
~OF DEBLIN~
316
~CITY OF WARSZAWA~
317
~CITY OF WILNO~
318
~CITY OF GDAŃSK~
BOMBER SQDNS
300
OF PROVINCE
~ZIEMIA MAZOWIECKA~
301
OF PROVINCE
~ZIEMIA POMORSKA~
304
OF PROVINCE
~ZIEMIA ŚLĄSKA~
305
OF PROVINCE
~ZIEMIA WIELKOPOLSKA~

BATTLE - BRITAIN
BATTLE of ATLANTIC
DIEPPE
WESTERN DESERT
ITALY
FRANCE
BELGIUM
HOLLAND

1940
1945

TO THE MEMORY OF
FALLEN POLISH AIRMEN

POLEGŁYM
LOTNIKOM POLSKIM

Above: *Plaque commemorating the sacrifice of the RAF during World War II.*

Left: *Memorial to the Polish airmen who fought with the RAF.*

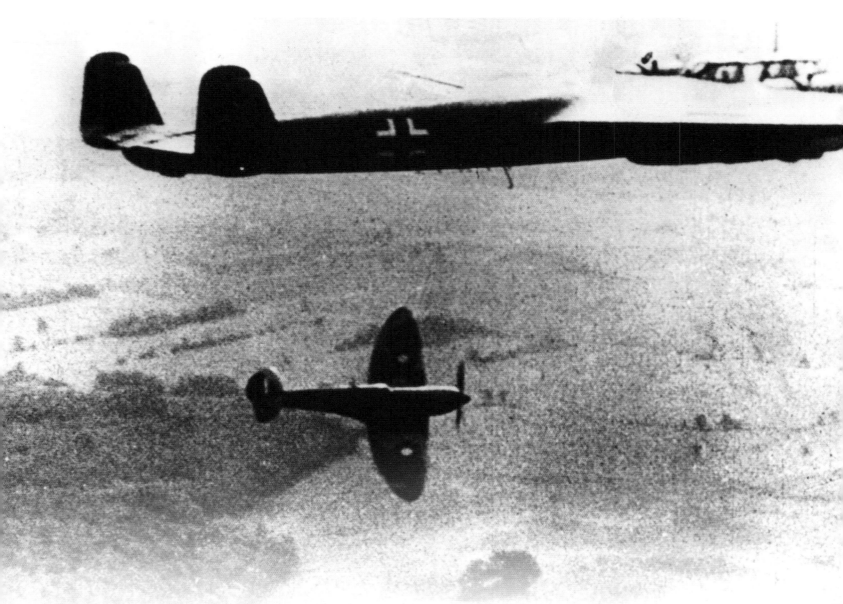

Above: A Spitfire takes on a Dornier Do17 "flying pencil" light bomber. Production of the Do17 stopped in the summer of 1940.

According to Fighting Area Tactics, RAF fighter pilots were to open fire at long range – 300 to 400 yards – then break off without closing in. However, when the Brownings fired, the wings flexed slightly, spreading the fire of, particularly, the outermost guns. At over 300 yards, fewer bullets were likely to hit the target. This was not so much of a problem in the Hurricane where the guns were mounted closer together. During the Battle of Britain, Spitfire pilots learned to open fire at 200 yards or less with their guns aimed inwards to concentrate fire at that range. This was a tactic the German pilots had adopted from the outset.

Polish pilots who had not been trained by the RAF flew in loose formations and opened fire from close range, becoming some of the most successful pilots of the war. Eventually, leaders such as "Sailor" Malan were instrumental in devising better tactics for the RAF fighters.

One disadvantage Bf 109 pilots faced was that, without long-range drop tanks, the plane could only fly for just over an hour. By the time they got over Britain, they had to keep an eye on a red fuel light. When it came on, they had to turn back and head for France. This limited their effectiveness escorting bombers or in combat.

The twin-seater Messerschmitt Bf 110 had a better endurance and was armed with two 20-mm cannon, four 7.92-mm machine guns in the forward fuselage, and one mounted in the rear cockpit for rear defence. However, they were not very manoeuvrable and proved to be sitting ducks for Spitfires and Hurricanes. After 18 August they were rarely seen over Britain as they were being shot down more quickly than they could be produced.

The Junkers Ju 88 bomber was difficult to shoot down. It was quite manoeuvrable and, especially at low altitudes with no bomb load, it could nearly outrun a Spitfire. Nearly 100 miles per hour slower than the Spitfire, the He 111 was easy to catch. However, it was heavily armoured and its self-sealing fuel tanks and progressively uprated defensive armament meant that it was still a challenge to shoot down. The Dornier Do17 was also easy to catch but, with its radial engines that had no vulnerable cooling systems and had self-sealing fuel tanks, it could take a huge amount of punishment. The Junkers Ju 87 Stuka dive bomber was completely outclassed and, after heavy losses, was withdrawn from the battle.

Below: This Spitfire has seen plenty of action, but young airmen could not wait to get her airborne again.

Douglas Bader

Having joined the RAF in 1928, two years later Bader lost both his legs in a flying accident while doing aerobatics and was cashiered. With the outbreak of war, Bader eventually managed to rejoin the RAF and scored his first kills over France and Dunkirk. During the Battle of Britain, he flew Hurricanes. In 1941, he was promoted Wing Commander and stationed at Tangmere. His unit was re-equipped with Spitfire Vbs, which had two Hispano 20-mm cannon and four .303 machine guns. However, Bader flew a Spitfire Va equipped with just eight .303 machine guns. These, he insisted, were more effective against enemy fighters. By August 1941 he claimed 22 kills, the fifth highest in the RAF.

On 9 August 1941, his plane was hit and he bailed out over France, losing a prosthetic leg in the process. In an agreement with the Luftwaffe, the RAF flew in a new one. He made numerous escape attempts, but was always recaptured and was eventually sent to Colditz Castle, the prison for incorrigible escapers. A mystery surrounds his downing. Bader claimed that he was the victim of a mid-air collision over Le Touquet. A Channel Four documentary claimed that he was shot down in a friendly fire incident. However, Luftwaffe pilot Max Meyer claimed the kill. When liberated in April 1945, he requested a return to action but this was refused. He left the RAF in February 1946.

From 1941 to 1943, the RAF began mounting attacks over Continental Europe, specifically to provoke a fighter response. However, they faced the same fuel-shortage disadvantage that the 109s had over Britain. By then the Luftwaffe had been re-equipped with the formidable new Bf 109F-1s and -2s. These easily outperformed the early Spitfires and matched the Mark Vs which were about to enter service. Luckily, a 109 F-2 crash-landed in a field near Dover on 10 July 1941. The Messerschmitt was repaired at Farnborough and used to upgrade the Spitfire.

During these sorties, five or more fighter squadrons flew in "circuses" above Blenheim or Stirling bombers. The Luftwaffe opposed these with relatively small numbers of fighters, inflicting disproportionate casualties. While leading the Tangmere Wing on a "circus" on 9 August 1941, the famous fighter ace Douglas Bader was shot down and captured.

Below: The most famous fighter pilot of the war, Squadron Leader Douglas Bader DSO DFC, commanding officer of 242 Squadron, perched on the cockpit of his Hurricane. Later he flew Spitfires.

Another type of operation flown by Fighter Command was the "rhubarb", a low-level ground attack mission by small numbers of fighters, usually under low cloud. After the Germans attacked Russia, they left behind a small cohort of experienced pilots as a rear guard. They were soon equipped with the Focke-Wulf Fw 190, which proved a formidable adversary until, on 23 June 1942, a Luftwaffe pilot landed by mistake at RAF Pembrey. In tests, it was found to be superior to the Mark Vb Spitfire, except in its turning radius. The Mark IX, introduced in July 1942, was found to be closely comparable. While, again, the Mark IX had a superior turning radius, it could be out-dived and out-rolled by the Focke-Wulf. As a result Rolls-Royce developed the Merlin 61 series engine into versions optimized for high, medium and low altitude performance, giving the prefixes HF, F, and LF to Marks VII through to IX Spitfires when the engine was installed. Mark V Spitfires also had their wing-tips removed and replaced with short fairings to improve their roll rate. These were known as "clipped, clapped and cropped Spits" as many had seen better days.

Below: *Ground crew service a Supermarine Spitfire LF Mk Vb of No 322 squadron at RAF Hawkinge – the cropped wing can be clearly identified here.*

The Focke-Wulf inflicted severe casualties on Spitfire V units and continued to be a serious threat even when the Mark IX was introduced. Focke-Wulf ace Hans "Assi" Hahn scored 53 of his 108 kills against Spitfires, while Josef "Pips" Priller scored 68 of his 101 kills against Spitfires, making him the highest-scoring Spitfire killer in the Luftwaffe. During the raid on Dieppe in August 1942, 88 Spitfires were lost, against 46 of all types of German aircraft. This led to a revision in tactics in the run-up to D-Day.

Focke-Wulf Fw 190

The Focke-Wulf Fw 190 is widely regarded as Germany's best fighter aircraft of World War II. It first appeared over France in early 1941 and was clearly superior to any other plane until the Spitfire IX, which took to the skies nearly a year later. Over 20,000 were built, including around 6,000 fighter-bomber models. Production continued until the end of the war and it was continually updated. Powered by a 2,100-horsepower BMW 801D-2 radial piston engine, it had a wingspan of 34 feet 5.5 inches. Its top speed was 408 miles per hour. It had a ceiling of 37,400 feet and a range of 500 miles. Standard armament included two 7.92-mm machine guns in the nose and up to four 20-mm machine guns in the wings. A wide range of bombs, guns and rockets was carried under the wings and fuselage.

Right: *The aircraft of a German pilot, seen at Pembrey, Carmarthenshire airfield, after being mistakenly landed there. This was the first intact Fw 190 to fall into Allied hands. It was immediately sent for flight trials to the Royal Aircraft Establishment, Farnborough.*

Numbers in the RAF were further depleted when the three Eagle squadrons – Americans flying Hurricanes, then Spitfire Vbs – left to become part of USAAF's Eighth Air Force.

Towards the end of September 1942, the Luftwaffe began launching high-level bombing raids against England with Junkers Ju 86R bombers flying at 40,000 feet. To counter this, RAF Northolt used a pair of Rolls-Royce Hucknall Spitfire IXs. These were converted Mark Vcs, stripped of everything inessential, lightening them by 450 lb. On 12 September 1942, Flying Officer Emanuel Galitzine intercepted a Junkers Ju 86R above Southampton at 41,000 feet. The ensuing battle soared to 43,000 feet, making it the highest air battle of the war. However, in the freezing air at that altitude the port cannon jammed. Whenever Galitzine fired, the aircraft would slew and fall out of the sky. The bomber escaped with just one hit to its port wing, but it was enough. Knowing they were now vulnerable, the Luftwaffe stopped its high-altitude raids.

Right: *A Spitfire of the USAAC evaluation team awaits trials at Freeman Field in Indiana, USA, towards the end of the war.*

Above: *Personnel of No 121 Eagle squadron look on as three Spitfire Vbs come in to land after a fighter sweep over northern France.*

Left: *A Spitfire Mark XIV, an upgraded Mark VIII with a Griffon 61 series engine, featuring a two-stage supercharger.*

In February 1943 the Rolls-Royce Griffon-engined Spitfire LF Mk XII entered service. These protected south-east England against low-level attacks and swept ahead of USAAF bomber raids over France, catching German fighters either on the ground or still climbing to intercept the bombers. However, because of the Spitfires' short range, their support was limited and their role was taken over by American fighters such as the P-47 Thunderbolt, P-38 Lightning and, from early 1944, the P-51 Mustang. The Spitfire only came back into its own after D-Day, when it could fly from airstrips in France.

Although the Spitfire suffered a hiatus in its usefulness as a fighter, it still had a role in photo-reconnaissance. Bristol Blenheims and Westland Lysanders had been detailed to carry out this task, but they were slow, lightly armed and suffered huge casualties. However, shortly before World War II started, Flying Officer Maurice Longbottom proposed that the RAF equip itself with small, unarmed aircraft which, stripped of unnecessary weight and equipped with cameras and extra fuel, could rely on high speed and altitude to evade enemy defences. The Spitfire was the ideal candidate. On 18 November 1939, flying from a base in France, Longbottom proved his theory by photographing Aachen from 33,000 feet. Although unarmed, Flying Officer George Patterson Christie, a reconnaissance Spitfire pilot, downed a Fiat BR20 bomber off the coast of Monaco on 13 June 1940 by repeatedly diving at it and forcing it to land in the sea. He was awarded the Distinguished Flying Cross.

Spitfires flew thousands of reconnaissance missions, usually ranging far into enemy territory and keeping up a continuous flow of information. In January 1941 a Photo-Reconnaissance Unit Spitfire took the first photographs of Germany's Freya radar. Later that year, Spitfire photographs taken from just 200 feet led to a raid on the radar station at Bruneval on the French coast, where vital components and radar operators were captured.

On photo-reconnaissance missions, pilots often flew for seven hours or more in the cramped cockpit of a Spitfire, which was unheated and unpressurized until later in the war. Photo-reconnaissance Spitfires usually had no radios. Even after they were added later, the pilot had to maintain radio silence throughout the flight. The pilot had to keep constant watch on the rear view mirror to make sure that a contrail would not give them away. Meanwhile he had to navigate by dead reckoning. Low-altitude missions were flown under low cloud, with the pilot constantly on the lookout for enemy fighters and flak positions. Once over the target they had to maintain a precise course and altitude. The slightest deviation would mean that the cameras might miss the target. A tiny black cross on the side of the canopy had to be lined up with a small black stripe painted on the aileron. Then, as the aircraft flew by the target, the pilot had to guess when to start photographing.

The first Spitfire to be posted in the Mediterranean was one from the Photo-Reconnaissance Unit, which arrived on Malta on 22 September 1941. It was then grounded for three weeks while awaiting replacements for its badly worn tyres. Three Mark IVs were sent to Vaenga, in North Russia, in September 1942 to keep an eye on German warships while Convoy PQ-18 was heading for Archangel. They carried Soviet markings and were later handed over to the Soviet Air Force.

Above: *Spitfires were assembled in Iraq for delivery to Russia. Here the guns are being tested before the planes are sent north.*

In March 1943, PRU Spitfires flying over Peenemunde showed that the Germans were developing rockets – the V-2 – which led to a bombing raid against the research establishment there. News of the development of the V-1 flying bomb led to photo-reconnaissance sorties over the Pas-de-Calais, where numerous launch ramps were sighted. These, too, were bombed. The Mark IX Spitfire from 1 PRU at Heston was also used to assess the success of the Dambusters raid of May 1943.

Spitfires saw action in other theatres during the war. The first batch of 15 Mark Vbs were taken to within flying distance of Malta by HMS Eagle on 7 March 1942. Others were ferried on board American carriers.

Right: *Reconnaissance photograph taken by a Spitfire of a V-1 site in northern France.*

Then in late October and early November, 12 Spitfire Vcs, equipped with 170-gallon drop tanks, flew direct from Gibraltar, a distance of 1,000 miles. They played a vital role in the defence of the island. The first Spitfire to be modified to carry underwing bombs was a Mark Vc based on Malta. It was adapted to carry a 250 lb bomb under each wing.

In North Africa, Spitfires were also used as tactical fighter-bombers. In the dusty conditions they carried a large air filter under the nose which increased drag and lowered performance. Later, the wings were strengthened for bomb-carrying and a new, smaller air filter was rigged up by RAF mechanics in Aboukir, Egypt. Later the longer-ranged Spitfire Mark VIIIs saw service with the RAF, South African Air Force and USAAF in Sicily and Italy. They were also given to the Italian air force, after Italy changed sides.

Above: *A Spitfire lands on the deck of the USS Wasp.*

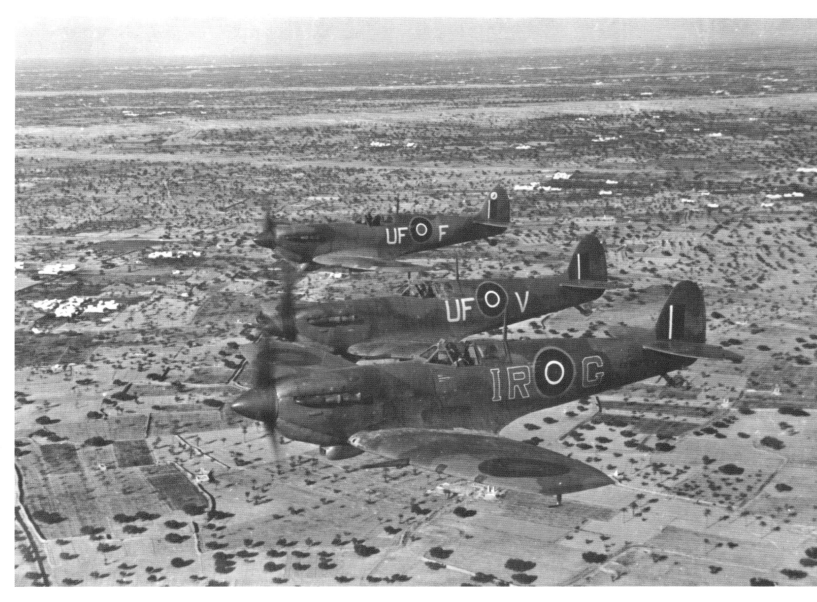

Above: *Spitfires above Djerba Island in the Gulf of Gabes off the coast of Tunisia. They are heading for the Mareth Line, where Rommel made his last stand against Montgomery in the desert war in 1943.*

Below: *A Spitfire in an anti-blast bay. Like all planes, the Spitfire was particularly vulnerable when it was on the ground.*

The Royal Australian Air Force, the Royal Indian Air Force and the RAF flew Spitfires against Japanese forces in the Pacific theatre. The first Spitfires in the Far East were two photo-reconnaissance planes which flew from airfields in India from October 1942. After the Japanese raid on Darwin in February 1942, Mark Vcs were sent there to be flown by Australian pilots who had seen action over North Africa.

Below: A Mark VIII HF Spitfire of the South African Air Force, with its Merlin 61 engine optimized for high-altitude flying, in Sicily on 3 October 1943.

Above: *Spitfires flew worldwide. This one is landing at Comilla in India (now Bangladesh), for use in the campaign against the Japanese in Burma.*

Above: *Spitfires flown by the RAF and Royal Australian Air Force above Port Darwin that fought off a Japanese attack there in 1943.*

Several Spitfires were lost before they learnt not to get into dogfights with Japanese Zeros. However, Spitfires were able to catch the Mitsubishi Ki-46 reconnaissance aircraft which flew high enough and fast enough to have evaded interception beforehand. In October 1943, the first Spitfire Mark VIIIs were sent to the RAAF to replace Spitfire Vcs, which were not ideally suited to the conditions there. But by then the Japanese air force had shifted its focus from the conquest of Australia to the defence of Japanese troops in the Solomon Islands and New Guinea.

Even though the Spitfire was not designed to fly in tropical conditions, it played a major part in the defence of Kohima and Imphal on India's border with Burma, protecting C-46 Commando transports which were resupplying the beleaguered 14th Army by air.

During the D-Day landings, Spitfires were used by both the US and Royal Navy as spotters, providing target coordinates and fire control for naval guns. After the Normandy landings, some Spitfires remained behind in England to counter the V-1 flying bomb offensive in mid-1944. Using new "150 Grade" fuel, their Merlin and Griffon engines could operate with higher boost pressures at lower altitudes. This meant they could catch V-1s and tip them off course with their wings, although this was a high-risk manoeuvre.

Right: Once the Allies established a beachhead in Normandy in June 1944, Spitfires and Mustangs flew from airstrips there to support the ground troops. Here the newspapers delivered from England that day are being distributed to the ground crew.

Below: A 500-lb bomb is being delivered to a Spitfire on a monsoon-sodden airstrip in Burma in 1945.

But the bulk of the Spitfire squadrons were moved across the Channel, operating as part of the 2nd Tactical Air Force from forward airfields close to enemy lines. Once the Allied air forces had achieved air supremacy, they were used in the fighter-bomber role, roaming over German territory, attacking targets of opportunity and providing ground support to army units. The Spitfire was not well suited to this role as the Merlin's glycol cooling system was particularly vulnerable to small arms fire. One well-aimed bullet could cause the engine to seize. As losses mounted, they were switched to giving high-altitude cover for low-to-medium altitude fighters, a role they were better suited for.

After the war the Swedish Air Force used Spitfires on photo-reconnaissance missions over Finland and the Soviet Union as no Russian fighter at the time could match its altitude until the mid-1950s. They remained in service with the Italian air force, who used them in air races. Spitfires were used by the Indian Air Force against invading forces in Kashmir in the 1947 Indo-Pakistan War. They saw their last combat in the 1948 Arab-Israeli War, where former RAF pilots flew Israeli air force Spitfires against the Spitfires of the Egyptian air force. Some air forces retained Spitfires in service well into the 1960s.

Below: *Ground crews ready Spitfires of the Second Tactical Air Force in Britain to support the Allied troops landing in Normandy.*

Thank You, Spitfires

Signal from General Anderson commanding VIII Bomber Command of the Eighth US Army Air Force to the Spitfires of Tangmere Wing, 15 July 1943: "American bomber crews are enthusiastically grateful for the splendid fighter cover provided today by the Spitfire pilots of your command. Following are typical comments of our crews: 'As we were leaving the target area a heavy formation of enemy fighters flew in to attack but almost immediately they were chased off by a particularly strong formation of Spitfires. On the way home about mid-Channel one of our ships with half its tail blown off dropped out of formation. A couple of Spits went to the aid of the crippled bomber immediately, circled the ship and brought her home safely.' 'The Spit cover was perfect,' exclaimed Captain Carrol D. Briscoa. 'I'd like to thank them personally.' May I add my grateful appreciation to that of our crews for the splendid co-operation of your command."

Longest Flight

A privately owned Spitfire was hired to do aerial photography for the Argentine government. Using external wing tanks and a belly ferry tank, wartime pilot James Elwyn Storey flew the Spitfire from Bournemouth to Gibraltar, then to Dakar in Senegal, Natal in Brazil, Rio de Janeiro and Porto Alegre, finally arriving in Buenos Aires. On the way, he established two records: one for the heaviest fuel load ever carried by a Spitfire and one for the longest flight for a Spitfire – the Dakar to Natal leg of approximately 1,870 miles.

Speed and Altitude Records

Beginning in late 1943, a Spitfire XI was used in high-speed diving trials at Farnborough to investigate the handling characteristics of aircraft travelling at speeds near the sound barrier. Flown by Squadron Leader A.F. Martindale, it reached a speed of 606 miles per hour – Mach 0.891 – in a 45-degree dive. Jeffrey Quill noted it was remarkable that "any operational aircraft off the production line, cannons sprouting from its wings and warts and all, could readily be controlled at this speed when the early jet aircraft such as Meteors, Vampires, P80s could not". However, on 5 February 1952, Flight Lieutenant Ted Powles, on a routine flight to survey outside air temperatures over Hong Kong, took his Spitfire to 51,550 feet, the highest recorded altitude ever achieved by a Spitfire. When the cabin pressure fell below a safe level, he tried to reduce altitude and went into an uncontrollable dive. He eventually regained control somewhere below 3,000 feet and landed safely. From the flight data it seems that, in the dive, he reached a speed of 690 mph – Mach 0.94 – the highest speed ever reached by a propeller-driven aircraft.

Chapter 9

Variants

There were 24 marks of Spitfire and numerous sub-variants. They came either with Merlin or Griffon engines, with various types of wing and in fighter, fighter-bomber and high speed photo-reconnaissance variants. The most common type was the Spitfire Mark V, which replaced the Mark I and II in 1941. Some 6,487 were built. The next most common airframe was the Mark IX, introduced to combat the Focke-Wulf Fw 190 – 5,665 were produced.

Different wings, featuring a variety of weapons, were fitted to most marks. The A wing carried eight .303-calibre machine guns. The B wing had four .303 machine guns and two 20-mm Hispano cannon, while the C or "universal" wing which could mount either four 20-mm cannon or two 20-mm cannon and four .303-inch machine guns. As the war progressed, the C wing became more common. The final armament variation was the E wing which housed two 20-mm cannon and two .50-inch Browning heavy machine guns.

Left: *Spitfires lined up at RAF Duxford in Cambridgeshire.*

The prototype Spitfire was powered by a 990-horsepower Merlin C engine. This was replaced by the 1,030-horsepower Merlin II in the Mark I production model. In all, 1,567 Mark Is were built. Many were adapted for photo-reconnaissance. The photo-reconnaissance version had the armaments, radio and all unnecessary equipment stripped out. The airframe was then rubbed down and repainted. High-altitude Photo-Reconnaissance Unit Spitfires were painted "PRU blue" – a dark blue-grey – while those used on low-level missions used pale "camoutint pink" which provided better camouflage against low cloud.

The first, the Mark I PR Type A, had cameras installed in the inner gun ports and heated to prevent the mechanism freezing or the lens misting at high altitudes. The gunsight was replaced by a camera control box. The PR Spitfires had "blown" canopies that featured large blisters to give the pilot a better view to the rear and below.

Above: *A Spitfire Mark I, of which 1,567 were made, many adapted for photo-reconnaissance.*

The Mark I PR Type B had a larger upgraded camera in the fuselage behind the pilot. An extra fuel tank was installed in the rear of the fuselage in place of the lead weights use to balance the constant-speed propeller units. The Type C had a larger fuel tank behind the pilot and another blister tank under the port wing, balancing the camera unit under the starboard. The plane could fly as far as Kiel in Germany.

Left: *Only the early prototype had a two-blade rotor. This was replaced in the production model with a three-blade rotor, then four.*

Above: *A Spitfire Mark I of B Flight, Number 19 Squadron based at RAF Duxford.*

Right: *K9942 – a Spitfire Mark I – first took to the air on 21 April 1939 and was delivered to 72 Squadron three days later. Its combat service ended on 5 June 1940 after an accident when landing at Gravesend.*

The Type D put more fuel in the leading edges of the wings and used the more powerful Merlin 45 engine. It could reach Stettin (Szczecin) in Poland. The Type E was modified for low-level photo-reconnaissance and had two cameras angled at 15 degrees below the horizontal in the wings. The Type F was a super-long-distance version built as an interim while the Type D was going into production. It could overfly Berlin. It became so useful that most Type Bs and Type Cs were converted and later models used the Mark V airframe. The Mark I PR Type G was used for fighter-reconnaissance missions, carrying eight .303 Browning machine guns, as well as having two cameras – one vertical, one oblique – and an extra fuel tank in the fuselage behind the pilot. The PR Mark VIII was a Type G with a Merlin 32 engine. Twenty-six were made from Type Gs, Mark IIs or Mark Vs for low-level armed reconnaissance missions in the run-up to D-Day.

A special sprint version of the Mark I Spitfire had been made in 1938 for an attempt on the World Speed Record. Its wings were shortened. It had flush rivets throughout and a highly polished finish, and a four blade propeller was added. But the speed record was quickly broken by a Heinkel He100, then a Messerschmitt Me209 at speeds the Spitfire could not match. So it was modified as a photo-reconnaissance plane – PR Mark II – but it only had a limited fuel capacity and was used as a liaison plane during the war.

The Spitfire Mark II had an upgraded Merlin XII engine and was made exclusively at Castle Bromwich. The Mark IIa carried eight Browning machine guns, the IIb had two 20-mm cannon and four Brownings. In early 1941, a number were converted to "long-range" Spitfires with a 40-gallon fuel tank installed under the port wing that inhibited manoeuvrability. When they were taken out of frontline service, 50 were converted for air-sea rescue work. A Merlin XX engine was fitted, along with flare chutes and marker bombs under the port wing. This was the Mark IIc, also known as the ASR Mark II. In all, 921 Mark IIs were built.

The Mark III was the first attempt to give the Spitfire an overall redesign. The Merlin XX engine was fitted and the wingspan and area reduced. The tailwheel became fully retractable and a bullet-proof panel was added to the canopy. Only one Mark III was made as it was decided to allocate the Merlin XX to the Hurricane. A prototype Merlin 61 was then installed, making it the Mark IX.

Above: A Mark II Spitfire, built at Castle Bromwich.

Left: Squadron Leader D.O. Finlay, Commanding Officer of No 41 squadron and former British Olympic hurdler, stands by his Spitfire Mk IIa. Part of the "Observer Corps" based at Hornchurch, Essex.

Above: *Supermarine developed a two-seater Mark VIII Spitfire for training. Adapted from a standard airframe, it got its certificate of airworthiness in January 1947.*

Right: *A Spitfire Mark V, of which 4,489 were built at Castle Bromwich.*

Anticipating pressurized Junkers Ju86P that could conduct high-level bombing missions over Britain, work began on the pressurized Spitfire. As a stop gap the Mark V was developed with a Merlin 45 series engine. The Mark Va had an A-type wing; the Mark Vb had a B wing and the Mark Vc, the C or "universal" wing. But in August 1941, these found themselves outclassed by the Focke-Wulf Fw 190 and were shipped overseas.

The Mark VI had a pressurized cabin, a four-blade propeller and extended Type B wings. Only 100 were made as the high-altitude bombing campaign did not materialize. The Mark VII was also pressurized. It used the larger Merlin 61 engine, which meant the nose had to be extended by seven inches. It also had pointed wing extensions – but on the Type C wing – used for high-altitude flying. These were later removed.

The Mark VIII was a Mark VII without the pressurized cabin. It came in low-altitude LF, medium altitude F and high-altitude HF versions, powered by Merlin 66, Merlin 63 and Merlin 70 engines respectively. Some had extended wingtips. With a 170-gallon drop tank, it could fly over 1,500 miles. Some had four 20-mm cannons; others carried up to 1,000 lbs of bombs under the wings or on a central bomb rack.

The Mark IX was a Mark Vc with a Merlin 61 engine and was found to be effective against the Focke-Wulf Fw 190. It was a high-level Mark IX with a polished PRU finish that incepted the Ju86R at 41,000 feet over Southampton. Low altitude LF, medium altitude F and high altitude HF versions with Merlin 66, Merlin 63 and Merlin 70 engines were made. Some were given the new E-type wing. And some Mark IXes and Mark XVIes were fitted with rockets under their wings. The Mark XVI was essentially a Mark IX with a Merlin 266 engine – a Merlin 66 built under licence by Packard in the US.

Above: *A Spitfire Mark IX at the Walney Island air show.*

Above: *A Spitfire Mark IX in the colours of the Irish Air Corps.*

Left: *Spitfire Mk Vc, fitted with a Rolls-Royce Merlin 45 engine. This aircraft was the first to be fitted with an experimental overload fuel tank, clearly seen under the the main body of the aircraft.*

Fifteen Mark XIs were taken off the production line to convert into photo-reconnaissance planes. A high-level PR Mark IX was used to photograph the Moehne dam after the Dambuster's raid. Armed low-level FR Mark IXs in "camoutint pink" were used to support army operations after D-Day. Several were used on photo-reconnaissance missions over Arnhem prior to Operation Market Garden.

The PR Mark XI combined the features of earlier versions. Around 471 were made. Perversely, the Mark X – essentially a Mark XI with a pressurized cabin – followed it into production. Only 16 were produced. The PR Mk XIII was an improved Type G with an old single-staged Merlin engine.

Below: *A Spitfire, paint-ready for the D-Day landings. During Operation Overlord, aircraft were painted with alternate black and white stripes for increased recognition in the hope of minimizing shootdowns due to "friendly fire".*

Below: Built at Castle Bromwich in 1941, Spitfire AB910 had a remarkable front-line operational career spanning almost 4 years. The aircraft was initially allocated to 222 (Natal) Squadron at North Weald on 22 August 1941 but was soon re-allocated to 130 Squadron. It flew several convoy patrols and also escort patrols to the daylight bombing raids against the battle cruisers Scharnhorst and Gneisenau in December 1941. AB910 is presented here as Spitfire Mk Vb, EN951 RF-D, the aircraft of Squadron Leader Jan Zumbach, officer commanding No. 303 (Kosciuszko) Squadron in 1942.

The Mark XII was a Mark VI with a Rolls-Royce Griffon engine. It first flew on August 1942, but only five were in service by the end of the year. It could reach 400 miles per hour in level flight and climb to an altitude of 30,000 feet in under eight minutes. Although the Spitfire continued to improve in speed and armament, range and fuel capacity remained major handicaps except in the photo-reconnaissance versions, where the armaments were replaced by extra fuel tanks.

Initially the Griffon engine only has a single-stage supercharger which gave it poor performance at high altitudes. The addition of the two-stage Griffon 61 series to the Spitfire Mark VIII resulted in the Mark XIV. Of the 957 Mark XIVs, 430 were low-level armed reconnaissance FR Mark XIV versions.

Above: A Spitfire Mark XII in 1942.

Left: A prototype Spitfire Mark XII with a Rolls-Royce Griffon engine replacing the Merlin.

Newer Griffon-engined Spitfires were being introduced as home-defence interceptors, where limited range was not an impediment. These faster Spitfires were used to defend against incursions by high-speed "tip-and-run" German fighter-bombers and V-1 flying bombs.

As long-ranged American fighters took over the long-distance escorting of USAAF daylight bombing raids, the Griffon-engined Spitfires progressively took up the tactical air superiority role as interceptors, while the Merlin-engined variants – mainly the Mark IX and the Packard-engined XVI – were adapted to the fighter-bomber role.

Below: *A Spitfire Mark XIV above the cloud base.*

Below: Rear view of a Spitfire FR Mk XVIII, which was fitted with a Rolls-Royce Griffon 65 or 66 engine.

Above: A Spitfire Mark XIV with a Merlin engine built under licence in the US by Packard.

Although the later Griffon-engined marks lost some of the favourable handling characteristics of their Merlin-powered predecessors, they could still out-manoeuvre their main German foes and other, later American and British-designed fighters. The distinctive Merlin sound of a supercharger whine and the accompanying whistle from the under-wing radiators was replaced by a deeper, throatier growl.

Marks XV and XVII were reserved for the naval version of the Spitfire – the Seafire. The Mark XVIII was a Mark XIV with stronger wings and larger fuel capacity. Like the Mark XIV it also came in a fighter-reconnaissance version. It came off the production line after the war, but some 300 were used in the Malayan Emergency.

The Mark XIX was the last photo-reconnaissance version of the Spitfire, with a pressurized cabin and a fuel capacity of 256 gallons; three-and-a-half times that of the original Spitfire. It came off the production line in May 1944 and was still in service in 1963.

Above: *A Spitfire Mark XVIII with a Rolls-Royce Griffon engine, featuring a two-stage supercharger, improving its performance at high altitude.*

Right: *A Spitfire LF 16E of central gunnery school.*

Mark XX, confusingly, was given to the original Mark IV Griffon-engined prototype. The Mark XXI was a development of the Mark XIV. Although it was generally thought to be unsatisfactory, 120 were produced. They only came off the production line in January 1945, so had little time to prove themselves in combat, though two claimed to have shot up a German midget submarine. Some 272 of the improved Mark XXII were produced, using features borrowed from the Supermarine Spiteful, the Spitfire's intended successor. More features from the Spiteful were incorporated in the Mark 24, though it was never produced. The last version, the Mark XXIV, was essentially a Mark XXII with two fuel tanks installed in the rear of the fuselage and fittings for rockets under the wings. Some 81 were made, of which 27 were converted Mark XXIIs. They saw services with the RAF until 1952 and with the Hong Kong Auxiliary Air Force until 1955.

Trainers

Supermarine also developed a two-seat T Mark VIII Spitfire for training. No orders were received for the trainer and only one was ever built. However, a number of unofficial two-seater airframes were rigged up in the field. In North Africa, a second seat was fitted in front of the cockpit of an RAF Mark Vb, replacing the upper fuel tank. This was not a dual-control trainer, simply a squadron run-about that could carry a passenger. Dual-controls were fitted to a small number of Mark IXs sent to Russia under the lend-lease programme. Known as a Mark IX UTI, it dispensed with the bubble canopy of the T Mark VIII, using instead an inline, framed, greenhouse-style double canopy.

After the war, Supermarine converted old Mark IX airframes to have a second raised cockpit with a bubble canopy. These TR9 variants were then sold to the Indian Air Force and the Irish Air Corps. Today, only a handful of the trainers are known to exist. They include a T Mark VIII and a T Mark IX based in America, and a privately owned TR9 that operates out of Duxford. However, its raised second cockpit has been lowered and now sits below the level of the front cockpit.

Left: *A Spitfire XVIII taking off at Duxford.*

The Seafire

The Seafire was a naval version of the Spitfire adapted for operation from aircraft carriers. It was fitted with folding wings and an arrester hook. The carrier equipment added to the weight and reduced the low-speed stability for which the Spitfire was known. Poor visibility over the nose and the narrow undercarriage track hampered deck operations. Early marks of Seafire had relatively few modifications, but late marks were heavily adapted.

The Seafire II was able to outperform the Zero at low altitudes in mock combat exercises. However, purpose-built carrier fighters such as the F6F Hellcat and F4U Corsair were more robust and practical for carrier operations. But the Seafire managed to regain its edge when the Griffon engine supplanted the Merlin towards the end of the war.

Left: A trainer in the colours of the Irish Air Corps. A two-seater was used to take the 91-year-old Alan Henshaw, the former Spitfire test pilot, on a memorial flight on 5 March 2006.

Below: A Seafire Mark III in 1942.

Spitfire Floatplanes

Things came full circle for Supermarine when Germany invaded Norway in April 1940 and the RAF took an interest in floatplane fighters that could be used where airfields were not immediately available. It was found that Spitfire Mark Is could work on floats, provided the vertical tail surfaces were enlarged as counter-balance. However, with the end of the Battle of Norway, the RAF needed all the Spitfires it could get so the prototype was converted back to an ordinary fighter.

When Japan came into the war the concept was revived. In early 1942 a Spitfire Vb was fitted with a 25-foot 7-inch pair of floats, mounted on cantilever legs. It was first flown by Jeffrey Quill on 12 October 1942. It had a top speed of 324 miles per hour at 19,500 feet. The maximum climb rate was 2,450 feet a minute at 15,500 feet, with an estimated ceiling of 33,400 feet.

Two more Vbs were converted and the three floatplanes were taken to Egypt, arriving in October 1943. At the time it was thought that the floatplanes could operate from concealed bases in the Dodecanese Islands and attack transport aircraft supplying German outposts in the area. The plan failed when the Germans overran the British-held islands of Kos and Leros. No other role could be found for them and they languished on the Great Bitter Lake in Egypt.

In the spring of 1944, a Spitfire IX was converted for use in the Pacific theatre, using the same components as the early conversions. Jeffrey Quill wrote: "The Spitfire IX on floats was faster than the standard Hurricane. Its handling on the water was extremely good and its only unusual feature was a tendency to 'tramp' from side to side on the floats, or to 'waddle' a bit when at high speed in the air." Soon after testing started, the idea of using floatplane fighters was dropped and the prototype was converted back to a landplane.

Below: Although the design of the Spitfire had evolved from a seaplane, when floats were added, little use was found for it.

Wing Types

The Spitfires with the Single Stage Merlin engines used five different wing types, which had the same dimensions and plan but different internal arrangements of armaments and fuel tanks. All Mark Is, IIs and Vs had small, rectangular undercarriage indicator pins which projected at an angle from the upper wing surfaces when the undercarriage legs were locked down. These supplemented lights on the instrument panel.

The A type was the original wing design, the basic structure of which was unchanged until the C type in 1942. Soon after production, heating for the gun bays was incorporated. Ducting drew hot air from the back of the radiators through the wings. The only armament able to be carried was eight .303-inch Browning machine guns which could freeze and jam at high altitudes.

Left: *The C-type "universal" wing was structurally modified to reduce labour and manufacturing time while allowing mixed armament options.*

Below: *Later Spitfires had their wing tips removed and replaced with short fairings to improve their roll rate.*

Wing Types (cont.)

B type was the A type that had been modified to carry a 20-mm Hispano cannon. The retractable underwing landing lamp was repositioned and the innermost machine-gun bays were replaced with a single cannon bay. The upper and lower wing skins incorporated blisters to clear the ammunition drum.

C type was the "universal" wing that was structurally modified to reduce labour and manufacturing time. It also allowed a mixture of machine guns and cannon to be carried. The undercarriage was redesigned, eliminating the upper-wing blisters over the wheel wells and landing gear pivot points and making the Spitfire more stable on the ground, reducing the likelihood of the aircraft tipping on to its nose.

D type was designed for unarmed long-range reconnaissance versions where the D-shaped wing structures ahead of the main spar converted into fuel tanks.

E type was a modified C wing carrying two 20-mm cannon and two .50-inch Browning heavy machine guns.

Starting with the Mark V, some Spitfires had their rounded wingtips replaced by shorter, squared-off fairings to improve low-altitude performance and enhance the roll rate. These are sometimes referred to as "LF" versions. This designation referred to the low-altitude version of the Rolls-Royce Merlin engine. While many "LF" Spitfires had "clipped" wings, some did not.

The Seafire version of the Spitfire had folding wings to fit in carrier hangars, and the conversion of the Spitfire Mark XIV – the Spiteful – had straight-tapering, laminar-flow wings like those on the P51 Mustang.

Left: The B-type wing had blisters on the upper and lower surfaces to allow room for the ammunition drums of its 20-mm Hispano cannon.

The Daimler-Benz Powered Spitfire Vb

In November 1942 a Spitfire Vb made a forced landing in a turnip field on German-occupied Jersey. The pilot, Free French flier Bernard Scheidhauer, was captured and was eventually shot in March 1944 for his part in the "Great Escape". The plane was taken to the Luftwaffe research facilities at Rechlin, where it was repaired and test flown with German markings. At the Daimler-Benz flight testing division in Echterdingen, south of Stuttgart, the Merlin engine was removed and replaced with a Daimler-Benz 605 engine from a Messerschmitt Bf109G, along with the propeller unit and supercharger air intake. The British 12-volt electrical system was replaced with a German 24-volt system, and the British instruments replaced by German ones. The Daimler-Benz Spitfire started flying in early 1944. The Spitfire was popular with German pilots and was flown regularly until it was destroyed by the USAAF in a bombing raid on 14 August 1944.

Left: A formation of Mark XII Spitfires with clipped wings for long-level flying. They also featured a new pointed rudder and a modified nose housing for the Griffon engine.

Rolls-Royce Griffon

Although the Griffon entered service long after the Merlin, it was essentially an older design, based on the Buzzard which first ran in 1928 and which itself was a scaled-up version of the Kestrel. The big Buzzard engine ran at only 2,000 rpm and was mostly used to power flying boats, but was developed into the R engine, which ran at 3,400 rpm for short periods and powered the Supermarine S6 to victory in its Schneider Trophy wins in 1929 and 1931. An updated version of the R was being developed in 1933, but was dropped in favour of the Merlin. Work did not begin again until 1939, 10 years after the first R engine flew. The new engine, the Griffon, ran at 2,750 rpm, remarkably for a big engine.

The first Griffons had single-stage superchargers and were fitted to the Spitfire Mark XII. They arrived just in time to take on the Focke-Wulf Fw 190, which they out-performed at low levels. For high altitude a two-stage supercharger was needed. These were fitted to the Spitfire XIV and XVIII and put the Spitfire back in the forefront of fighter performance until the development of the jet.

The Griffon is a 12-cylinder, liquid-cooled, 36.7-litre upright V engine with a bore of 6 inches and a stroke of 6.6 inches. The Griffon II, with a single-stage supercharger, gave 1,720 horsepower at take-off, 1,730 horsepower at 750 feet and 1,490 horsepower at 14,000 feet. The Griffon 61, with a two-stage supercharger, gave 1,540 horsepower at take-off, but 2,030 horsepower at 7,000 feet and 1,820 horsepower at 21,000 feet.

Below: *A Spitfire Mark XIII with a Griffon engine.*

Right: *The Spitfire Mark XIV with a Griffon 65 engine that could develop up to 2,050 horsepower.*

Chapter 10
Survivors and Memorials

Left: *This Spitfire is on permanent display at the Imperial War Museum in Lambeth, South London.*

Left: *The Science Museum in South Kensington in London also has a Spitfire on display.*

THE JET AGE

There are some 44 Spitfires and a handful of Seafires that are still airworthy, though many museums such as Chicago's Museum of Science and Industry have others on static displays.

The Battle of Britain Memorial Flight at RAF Coningsby in Lincolnshire maintains and operates five Spitfires for flying display and ceremonial purposes. There are regularly more than a dozen Spitfires on site at Duxford. Some fly. Others are being restored or are on static display. Kennet Aviation, a British company specializing in restoring ex-military aircraft, has an airworthy Seafire XVII and a number of other Seafire restoration projects underway at its home airfield at North Weald Airfield in Essex. The Shuttleworth Collection in Bedforshire maintains and displays an airworthy Spitfire Mark Vc.

A Spitfire Mark IX currently flies from the former-RAF station at Biggin Hill. After the war it had been sold to the South African Air Force. Recovered from a scrapyard, it was returned to England in the early 1990s. It now wears 234 Squadron markings with coding FX-M. An airworthy Spitfire Mark XVI Spitfire is also on display at the Potteries Museum and Art Gallery in Hanley after being presented to the City of Stoke-on-Trent in 1969 to commemorate R.J. Mitchell's origins in the Potteries. A statue of Mitchell stands outside the museum.

Below: A Spitfire Mark XVI at Coningsby undergoing restoration.

The Temora Aviation Museum in New South Wales has two airworthy Spitfires – a Mark VIII and a Mark XVI – which fly regularly during the museum's flying weekends. The Mark VIII is painted with distinctive shark's teeth. One of the few Spitfires still in its original paint is displayed in the Australian War Memorial in Canberra. It has not been repainted since World War II.

Right: *R.J. Mitchell was born and brought up near Stoke and his life and achievements are commemorated in the museum there.*

Below: *An airworthy Mark XVI Spitfire is on display at the Potteries Museum and Art Gallery in Hanley after being presented to the City of Stoke-on-Trent.*

The **Spitfire** was an incredible, **immortal**

In 1956 New Zealander Sir Keith Park, the commander of No 11 Fighter Group during the Battle of Britain, arranged for a Spitfire Mark XVI to be donated to the Auckland War Memorial Museum, New Zealand, where it has been on display ever since.

A Spitfire LF Mark XVIe owned by the Subritzky family of North Shore, Auckland, was recently put up for sale. Built at Castle Bromwich in late April 1945, it is thought to be worth some £2 million. In 1957 it joined the Battle of Britain Memorial Flight. After being sold to the Smithsonian Institution in 1959, it was put on display in the USAF museum at Dayton, Ohio. In 1996 it was bought by a Hong Kong businessman, James Slade, who shipped it to Don Subritzky for restoration work in 1997, and the Subritzky family subsequently bought it.

Below: The Mark VIII Spitfire at Temora Aviation Museum in New South Wales is painted with distinctive shark's teeth.

Above: There are a number of Spitfire Mark IXs on display around the world – in Britain, Greece, Italy and California. This one is in the colours of the Dutch Air Force.

A Spitfire LF Mark XVIe is on display in the Polish Aviation Museum in Krakow. The Hellenic Air Force Museum has a Supermarine Spitfire Mk IXc, which it displays at Dekeleia Air Base. Another Spitfire Mark IX is on display at the Vigna di Valle Museum – Italy's Air Force Museum – at Bracciano, north of Rome.

Above: *American aircraft collector Kermit Weeks keeps a Spitfire Mark XVI at his Fantasy of Flight museum in Florida.*

A black-painted Spitfire is on exhibition in the Israeli Air Force Museum in Hazerim. It belonged to former president and RAF pilot Ezer Weizman, who flew a Spitfire during the Israeli War of Independence in 1948. The so-called Black Spitfire is used for ceremonial flying displays.

US aircraft collector Kermit Weeks keeps a Spitfire Mark XVI at his Fantasy of Flight museum in Florida, which claims to be the world's largest private aircraft collection. The plane was built in Castle Bromwich in 1945. After he bought it, Weeks insisted that it be restored to as close to its original condition as possible. Guns, cannons, gun sight and original working radios were re-installed and it is said to be "the most originally restored Spitfire in the world". Ezell Aviation, the Texas aircraft restorers, restored a Seafire 47 for US collector John Smith.

The Lone Star Flight Museum in Galveston, Texas, has a Spitfire Mark XVI which is in flying condition and carries the markings of Texan ace Lance C. Wade, who flew with the RAF from December 1940 until his death in an air accident in Foggia, Italy, in 1944.

The Fighter Factory in Suffolk, Virginia, has a 1943 Spitfire Mark IX that flew 15 sorties over Italy. It was found in a playground in Israel in the 1970s, when it was taken back to England for restoration. The collection belongs to Gerald Yagen, chief executive of Tidewater Tech vocational schools which aim to encourage students to take courses in aircraft maintenance.

Above: *This Spitfire, seen here flying over the Severn Bridge, belongs to the Rolls-Royce Heritage Trust.*

The Vintage Wings of Canada Collection at Gatineau, Quebec, has a Spitfire Mark XVI carrying the markings of No 421 Squadron Royal Canadian Air Force. The TAM Asas de Um Sonho (Wings of a Dream) Museum at São Carlos, Brazil, has the only airworthy Spitfire in South America. A Mark IXc built in 1943, it was restored in California and donated to the museum by Rolls-Royce. It is painted in the colours and markings of RAF ace James Edgar "Johnnie" Johnson. The highest-scoring pilot in the European theatre, Johnson shot down 34 confirmed enemy aircraft. He had seven shared victories, three shared probables, ten shared damaged and one destroyed on the ground.

The site of the main Spitfire factory at Castle Bromwich is commemorated by a sculpture called the Sentinel by Tim Tolkien, great-nephew of the author. It shows three half-size Spitfires peeling off in different directions, their curved steel supports appearing as vapour trails. At the entrance to Southampton International Airport – formerly Eastleigh Aerodrome which saw the first flight of the aircraft in March 1936 – there is a sculpture of the prototype. The site of the RAF base at Thornaby is marked by another Spitfire memorial. It is not far from a school named after Douglas Bader. A fibreglass replica of a Spitfire has been mounted on a pole in Memorial Park, Hamilton, New Zealand, as a tribute to all New Zealand fighter pilots who flew Spitfires in World War II.

Below: *The Vintage Wings of Canada Collection at Gatineau, Quebec, has a Spitfire Mark XVI carrying the markings of Number 421 Squadron, Royal Canadian Air Force.*

Below: A sculpture showing three half-size Spitfires peeling off in different directions, mounted on steel vapour trails, stands on the site of the main Spitfire factory at Castle Bromwich.

Below: Another statue of R.J. Mitchell can be found in the Solent Sky Museum in Southampton, where he did most of his important work.

Around the quadrangle at the centre of the RAF Museum, Hendon, England, are two replica aircraft, a Hurricane and this Spitfire (below). In the museum itself there are several Supermarine products, including this Spitfire (right).

Index

Acknowledgements

The Author and Publisher would like to thank the following people and organizations for their contribution to this book:

The quote from the speech made by Winston Churchill is reproduced with permission of Curtis Brown Ltd, London, on behalf of The Estate of Winston Churchill.
Copyright © Winston S. Churchill

Imperial War Museum, London, England.
Aeroplane Magazine, London, England.
The Spitfire Society, Biggin Hill, Westerham, England.
Tangmere Military Aviation Museum, West Sussex, England – for allowing us to photograph the Spitfire prototype replica.
US Library of Congress, Washington DC, USA.
US National Archives, Washington DC, USA.
Air Team Images – www.AirTeamImages.com
Peter Handley – Vintage Wings of Canada, Quebec, Canada (p.248).
Fantasy of Flight Museum, Polk City, Florida, USA (p.246).
Solent Sky Museum, Southampton, England.
Ian Craighead, Rolls Royce Heritage Trust.
Rolls-Royce Plc (p.249).
TopFoto Picture Library, Edenbridge, England.
ED Archives, Edgmond, Newport, England.
Cody Images, Beith, Scotland.
The British Library, London, England (p.84).

Front Cover – Alamy/Dave Pattison